SPIES *of*
REVOLUTIONARY
CONNECTICUT

SPIES *of* REVOLUTIONARY CONNECTICUT

From Benedict Arnold to Nathan Hale

MARK ALLEN BAKER

Charleston — London

THE
History
PRESS

Published by The History Press
Charleston, SC 29403
www.historypress.net

Front cover: Image of Benedict Arnold by artist John Trumbull. *Courtesy of the Library of Congress,*
LC-USZ62-68483; Nathan Hale by sculptor Larry Wasiele, Veterans' Memorial Green, Town
of Coventry, Connecticut, John Elsesser, Town Manager. *Photograph by the author.*
Back cover: Image of Bushnell's Turtle. *Courtesy of the Library of Congress, LC-USZ62-110384.*

First published 2014

Manufactured in the United States

ISBN 978.1.62619.407.6

Library of Congress CIP data applied for.

To Flavil Quinn Van Dyke III,
"...a man of high morals and character, who saw the good in all people and helped many of them achieve their true potential."
A Patriot in every sense of the word and a beloved friend.

In Memoriam
Ford William Baker and James Buford Bird

Contents

CONTENTS

Preface

Our cause was just. Our union was perfect. Our intelligence resources were so profound that they echoed from every rolling hill of our northeastern outpost. And when foreign assistance was deemed necessary, we had no further to look than Wethersfield.

"Join or Die," the well-known Benjamin Franklin cartoon published in his *Pennsylvania Gazette* on May 9, 1754. *LC-USZ62-9701.*

We gratefully acknowledged, as signal instances of the Divine favor toward us, that his Providence would not permit us to be called into this severe controversy until we were grown up to our present strength, had been previously exercised in warlike operation and possessed of the means of defending ourselves—conditions met by our state's provisions.

Our Connecticut, the epicenter of freedom, embraced its role. Our hearts fortified with these animating reflections, we most solemnly, before God and the world, declared that, exerting the utmost energy of these powers in all forms, which our beneficent Creator hath graciously bestowed upon us, the arms and intelligence we have been compelled by our enemies to assume, we did so, in defiance of every hazard, with resolve and perseverance. For the preservation of our free will; being with one Connecticut mind, hell-bent without restrain.

May God forever bless our Connecticut Patriots, their families and the ground that so welcomed their footsteps of freedom.[1]

Acknowledgements

This work owes a debt of gratitude to a wealth of individuals and institutions. To the staff at The History Press: Jeff Saraceno, Hannah Cassilly, Darcy Mahan and the entire production staff, I am so very grateful.

My sincerest appreciation to the following: the Town of Brooklyn; the Town of Carmel, New York; the Town of Coventry (John Elsesser); the Nathan Hale Homestead (Beverly York, site administrator); the Town of Essex; the Connecticut River Museum (Amy Trout, curator); the Griswold Inn; the Town of Lebanon (author and historian Alicia Wayland); Governor Jonathan Trumbull Home (Nancy A. Merwin, CTDAR, and Jessi Johnson); the Town of Norwich; the Leffingwell House Museum (Society of the Founders of Norwich, Connecticut); the Town of Wethersfield; the Webb-Deane-Stevens Museum; and the Town of Windsor.

My gratitude to the following Connecticut historical societies (alphabetical by town): Ashford Historical Society; Connecticut Historical Society; Hebron Historical Society (Mary-Ellen Gonci); Lebanon Historical Society Museum & Visitors Center (Donna Baron, director, and Grace Sayles, administrative assistant); Litchfield Historical Society, which includes the Reeve House and Law School and the Ingraham Library; Wethersfield Historical Society; and Windsor Historical Society (Connie Thomas, administrative assistant).

Also to the following libraries/museums: the Library of Congress; National Archives and Records Administration (NARA); the New York Public Library; the Smithsonian Institution; Beinecke Rare Book & Manuscript Library; Yale University, New Haven, Connecticut; and Musée et du Domaine National de

Versailles. And thanks to the United States Intelligence Community (IC), a federation of sixteen separate United States government agencies, especially the Central Intelligence Agency.

Editorial review provided by Matthew Robert Baker.

Connecticut inspiration provided by Dana Beck and Brian Brinkman, Kelly and Dennis DiGiovanni, Pete and Jackie Gulbrandsen, Ann and Mark Lepkowski, Jim Risley and Scott and Dianna Wallquist. Also thanks to Mark Brett, Steve Ike, Mark Williamson and Pennsylvania music historian Thomas R. Grosh.

My thanks to family: Marilyn Allen Baker, Aaron and Sharon Baker, Elizabeth Baker, Rebecca Baker and Brad Lane. Joined by my father-in-law, Richard Long, and my wonderful wife, Alison, I was fortunate enough to visit Normandy, France, on the sixty-ninth anniversary of D-Day. It was there that I saw these words from Sergeant John B. Ellery, U.S. First Infantry Division, etched in stone: "You can manufacture weapons and you can purchase ammunition but you can't buy valor and you can't pull heroes off an assembly line."

Freedom has a price. God bless our veterans!

Every Picture Tells a Story

S uspended inside the United States Capitol Rotunda is a twelve- by eighteen-foot oil-on-canvas filled with more brushstrokes of freedom than any presentation of its kind. Its majesty is a testament to its creator, artist John Trumbull. Underneath, a marquee reads, "Congress, at the Independence Hall, Philadelphia, July 4, 1776."

However, it, like much of the American Revolution, has become part of a collection of myths and misrepresentations.[2] The artist titled it *The Declaration of Independence* but mentioned nothing about a date, location (Pennsylvania Statehouse) or even if the scene ever took place. It did not.

Founder John Adams had lectured Trumbull on the importance of accuracy, stating, "Let not our posterity be deluded with fictions under the pretense of poetical or graphical license" in reference to the artist's historical commission. Veracity is the soul of righteousness, as Thomas Huxley would confirm, not creativity.[3]

Hailing from Pilgrim stock, the artist was born in the picturesque town of Lebanon, Connecticut, on June 6, 1756. The sixth child of Jonathan Trumbull, governor of Connecticut, and his wife, Faith Robinson Trumbull, he entered Harvard at age fifteen and graduated in 1773. His obsession for art engaged the eye of George Washington, who appointed him an aide-de-camp; Trumbull had meandered his way to view and then draw the British position at Boston Neck. Later, in 1777, he resigned his colonel's commission and turned back to the canvas.

John Trumbull's painting *Declaration of Independence*, depicting the five-man drafting committee presenting their work to the Congress. *LC-USZ62-115965.*

THE ARREST OF JOHN TRUMBULL

In the autumn of 1779, Trumbull took an artistic residency in Boston. There he became acquainted with John Temple, later Sir John, and first British consul-general to the United Sates. Viewed as politically neutral, the well-connected Temple was married to a daughter of Governor James Bowdoin. He was also acquainted with the noted Anglo-American painter Benjamin West, who was working in London; it would be Temple who would urge Trumbull to go there and study with the future president of the Royal Academy. Seeing both his military service and family name, naturally this suggestion struck Trumbull as being a bit peculiar, if not somewhat dangerous. Temple however, assured the young man that he could obtain the proper permission. And to his credit, he did precisely that, securing clearance from Lord George Germaine, the British secretary of state—not without conditions, however, that he would be watched and must avoid the smallest indiscretion.[4]

In the middle of May 1780, Trumbull boarded the French ship *La Negresse* bound for Nantes in western France. The journey would take about five weeks. The artist, complete with letter of introduction from Dr. Benjamin Franklin, then traveled to London to meet with West; it would be in West's studio where he would also encounter the celebrated portrait artist Gilbert Stuart.[5]

On November 15, 1780, news arrived in London of the treason of General Arnold and the execution of Major André. "Never perhaps did any man suffer death with more justice, or deserve it less," politician Alexander Hamilton penned on the hanging of André, an opinion shared by many but a price paid by one. So revered in Great Britain was the British spy that his remains—originally buried under the gallows where he met his fate—were removed to England in 1821 and placed in a section of the South Transept of Westminster Abbey known as Poet's Corner. Conscious that André had been the deputy adjutant general of the British army, and that he himself held the identical position in America, Trumbull couldn't have expressed himself better when he said, "It seemed to them that I should make the perfect pendant."[6]

Trumbull was ordered to be secured, with papers, for examination and threatened with hanging as an American spy. "A thunderbolt falling at my feet, would not have been more astounding, for conscious of having done nothing politically wrong, I had become as confident of safety in London, as I should have been in Lebanon," he would later recall.[7] Conducted first

The home of Governor Jonathan Trumbull and his family in Lebanon, New London County. *LC-024538p.*

15

to detention at the Brown Bear in Drury Lane, the artist would contemplate his fate.

Accused of bearing arms against the king, he was remanded to lockup. From Tothill Fields Bridewell Prison—a stark contrast to Newgate, the former London prison notorious for its unsanitary conditions in the eighteenth century—Trumbull was given the prison allowance and permitted to pay for additional privileges.

Thankfully, through Benjamin West a message was given Trumbull from the king "that, in the worst possible event of the law, his life shall be safe."[8] After a close confinement of seven months, the prisoner was admitted to post bail with the condition that he should leave the kingdom in thirty days and not return until after peace should be restored. Trumbull, determined to return home through the shortest route, quickly headed to Amsterdam, joined in transit by a sympathetic John Temple.

In Amsterdam, Trumbull found housing under the roof of a Mr. De Neufville, a supporter of the American cause. While imprisoned, the Patriot had been visited by De Neufville's son, at which time Trumbull requested that they retain any letters that might come into their hands addressed to him—a wise protection mechanism. Inside one of the held missive packets, Trumbull surprisingly found authority and instructions to negotiate a loan with Holland for the State of Connecticut.[9] Peculiar, so the Patriot thought. Following consultation with emissary John Adams, whom he had met in Amsterdam, the request was abandoned. Baffled at every point, the artist decided to resume his journey home.

After the war, Trumbull returned to London to paint *his* view of the Revolution, the canvas court now both judge and jury. There would be no preconditions associated with his work; artistic license, like revolution, has no bounds. While there is an endearing romance associated with the artist's work, the American Revolution was never as inviting or prepossessing as Trumbull's fluid brushstrokes and subtle glosses.[10] After all, "without art," as George Bernard Shaw would later quip, "the crudeness of reality would make the world unbearable."

Paint your own picture; that's the Connecticut mindset.

I. Probable Cause

Chapter 1

In Pursuit of Freedom

The American Revolution in Connecticut

To be prepared for war is one of the most effective means of preserving peace.
—*George Washington*

That preparation would fall largely to the colony of Connecticut. It was a role the Provision State assumed with pride, for its greatest supply was that of intelligence.

Connecticut's rich heritage, seeded by the culture of its Native Americans, drew its strength from six key elements. Administration was the first. The charter granted by Great Britain's Charles II, combined with the management provided by Jonathan Trumbull, the last colonial administrator (1769–76) and the only such principal to light the torch of the Patriot cause, provided regional autonomy. Colonization, or the vigorous variety of Puritanism, and communication added to the mix. Located along the Post Road system, Connecticut was home to New Haven's *Gazette* (1755) and Hartford's *Courant* (1764). Home to one of the nine colonial colleges, the Collegiate School (which eventually became Yale University), founded and chartered in 1701, would have an enormous impact on the ideology of the time and solidify education as another factor.[11] Militarization, or an effective early militia, and location completed the mix. Between two hotbeds of liberty, Boston and New York, Connecticut proved the perfect epicenter.

The Connecticut Colony—what would be the fifth state admitted to the Union on January 9, 1788—had over 150 years to plant its roots firmly in New England. This heritage, combined with the actions that follow, affected

A spectacular landscape view looking north from Mountain Road in Farmington, Connecticut. *LC-222696p.*

residents, lending provocation to their endeavors, which in some cases meant intelligence gathering. And, as we will later see, it was not always for whom you might think.

PRUDENCE: 1763–1774

British spending during the French and Indian War (1754–63) and the decade that followed created a staggering revenue void.[12] It was now time, so our sovereign believed, for its North American colonies, the beneficiaries of that freedom, to contribute to its maintenance.

Having endured under English navigation acts and the Molasses Act of 1733, the colonists then faced a settlement restriction, the Royal Proclamation of 1763, followed by additional forms of provocation in the Sugar Act, Currency Act, Quartering Acts and Stamp Act of 1765. The latter and most contentious— having been the first direct tax levied—of the bunch was thankfully repealed.

However, the Declaratory Act of 1766 soon followed. Obvious now was the redundant pattern of oppression, and there was no relief in sight.

British persistence, never at a loss, came next in the form of one Charles Townshend and his despotic laws. The Townshend Acts—commonly considered to be the Revenue Act of 1767, the Indemnity Act, the Commissioners of Customs Act, the Vice Admiralty Court Act and the New York Restraining Act—met with even greater resistance in the

The Bloody Massacre Perpetrated in King Street, Boston, on March 5th, 1770, by Paul Revere. *LC-USZC4-110.*

colonies. Resistance was so strong that it prompted British occupation. Connecticut governor William Pitkin, who died in office and was succeeded by Deputy Governor Jonathan Trumbull, protested the Townshend Acts; it was a rather incongruous and bold position. Meanwhile, in the eastern part of the colony, the surreptitious Sons of Liberty urged a boycott of British goods.

Enter the most famous snowball fight in New England history: the Boston Massacre of March 5, 1770. Five civilian men were killed and six others injured during a confrontation—primed by verbal threats and thrown objects, one of which was a snowball—with British troops stationed in the city. The root of this conflict was also answered, as duties under the Townshend Acts were repealed—except the tax on tea. The Tea Act, passed in 1773, imposed no new taxes but gave British merchants a monopoly on tea at the expense of their colonial counterparts. The colonists' retort was the "Destruction of the Tea in Boston," or what would later be called the Boston Tea Party, on December 16, 1773.

Ever watchful, the colony of Connecticut kept one eye on the state of affairs in the three adjoining colonies and the other on preparation for an impending struggle. It was a unique and auspicious position: not having

Benjamin Franklin before the lord's council, Whitehall Chapel, London, 1774. *LC-USZC4-5296.*

to battle against a thoroughly Crown-loyal governor allowed Connecticut colonists to focus their full attention on the oppressive measure of King George III and his draconian Parliament.

In response to the lost tea, again Parliament took action, this time in the form of the Intolerable (Coercive) Acts of 1774. They included: the Boston Port Act, Massachusetts Government Act and the Administration of Justice Act, and some scholars also include the Quebec Act.[13] Of the four, the Massachusetts Government Act was the most forceful; after a century and a half of local self-government, citizens just to the north of Connecticut were deprived a voice. In response, Massachusetts Patriots seized all political and military authority outside Boston by the fall of 1774. While historically overlooked, these actions proved a prelude to the inevitable.

The colonists also countered with an administrative response: the first of three Continental Congresses met on September 5, 1774. Delegates, fifty-six from twelve colonies (not including Georgia), met in Philadelphia to assess their situation. Connecticut sent Silas Deane, Eliphalet Dyer and Roger Sherman.

Deane we will address later. As for the lawyer, jurist and statesman Dyer, John Adams in his diary characterized him as "longwinded and roundabout, obscure and cloudy, very talkative and very tedious, yet an honest and trustworthy man."[14] Finally, lawyer, politician and founding father Roger Sherman was described by Thomas Jefferson as "Mr. Sherman, of Connecticut, a man who never said a foolish thing in his life."[15] The first mayor of New Haven, he was also was the only individual to sign all four great state papers of the United States: the Continental Association, the Declaration of Independence, the Articles of Confederation and the Constitution.[16]

This plaque commemorating the site of Roger Sherman's home appears at Yale University. It speaks for itself.

Ever prudent, Connecticut continued to aggressively legislate. A broadside—perhaps the most effective form of communication at the time—with its use of the long "s" and bold text proclaims: "'ACTS AND LAWS,' Made and paffed [passed, the first usage of the long 's'] by the General Court or Affembly of His Majefty's Englifh Colony of Connecticut, in New-England, In America."[17] This 1774 act was passed "for formulating and regulating the Militia, and for the Encouragement of Military Skill for the better Defence of this Colony." It directed regiment superiors to "collect the Fire-Arms and other Implements of War within their respective Regiments, which belong to this Colony, and cause them to be repaired and fitted for Use." Posted throughout the protectorate it was a dauntless directive!

On December 14, 1774, the General Assembly, with hopes of purchasing six hundred half-barrels of gunpowder, permitted mariner Nathaniel Shaw Jr. to send one of his vessels to the West Indies. The explosive combination of saltpeter, sulfur and charcoal had become a treasured composition.

The gravity of the situation was clear. Within the colony's vast geographical influence—extending north of Plainfield, New Hampshire, then south into New Jersey (Essex County) and eastern Long Long Island, then west to northeastern Pennsylvania, before heading north again to present-day Vermont—preparedness became paramount. True, the same flag flew over Hartford and London, separated by over three thousand miles and a vast ocean, yet it represented two diverse mindsets.

A Connecticut Calling: 1775

Eleven days after the Parliament of Great Britain declared the Province of Massachusetts Bay to be in rebellion on February 20, 1775, the House of Lords was the recipient of a plan for reconciliation with America from Lord North himself, the very minister whose policies had helped propel the colonists with thoughts of revolution. Following approval from the Lords and House of Commons, it was sent to America, where it arrived in Boston one day after the Battles of Lexington and Concord. The proposal was evidence that England, like the colonies, did not favor an armed conflict.[18]

Also on April 20, representatives from the Massachusetts Provincial Congress met at the home of Connecticut governor Jonathan Trumbull. They had come south with an urgent appeal for assistance to the Committee

Set of portraits depicting American Revolutionary War veterans who lived to be one hundred years old or more. *LC-DIG-ppmsca-3534.*

of Correspondence. Without falter, their neighbors answered their cry. As Trumbull insightfully noted, "The ardour of our people is such that they can't be kept back." Posthaste, Patriot militia from Connecticut, New Hampshire, Massachusetts and Rhode Island encircled Boston in significant numbers. Less than a week later, on April 26, the Connecticut General Assembly established a commissariat to provide supplies to forces in Boston. Joseph Trumbull, the governor's son, was appointed commissary general. Jonathan Trumbull Jr. was appointed paymaster of the army's Northern Department. The governor also recommended building a new fort to protect New London at Shaw's Neck.

Following a special session of the General Assembly in Hartford, six regiments composed of ten companies each were created. These six state brigades would become part of the Connecticut Army on June 14. In a preemptive measure, the assembly also created a Council of Safety to combat hostilities. Consisting of assembly members, the council would assist the governor in the defense of the colony. The guidance needed for both military and civilian efforts had been put in place.

When news of the Lexington bloodshed reached the Mortlake (now Pomfret) farm of Israel Putnam (1718–1790), the veteran officer left his plow in the field and rode straight through the night, traveling one hundred miles in eight hours, to Cambridge, leaving word to be followed by the local militia. Already a well-known hero, nothing spread faster along the Post Road than a parable of "Old Put," and there were many such tales, like his killing the last wolf in the colony to nearly being burned at the stake by Indians in the French and Indian War. Now there would be more. He then commanded Patriot forces during the Battle of Bunker Hill, where he received a commission as brigadier (later major) general in the Continental army. These actions were indicative of the outrage shared by colonial residents.[19]

The colony of Connecticut had had an organized militia system in place since 1739; it would be a concept that would continue into the 1840s. Made up of residents, these town companies would occasionally muster on the green or common to drill among themselves. But they would also train with their numbered regiments, which were commanded by field grade officers. When combined with militia brigades under the command of a brigadier general, they were formidable forces.

The Second Company of Governor's Foot Guard, composed of the sons of the leading New Haven families, was among the first Connecticut units to troop north in April 1775. In step with his countrymen was one Benedict Arnold. In Boston, he would soon take direction to Fort Ticonderoga, a British-held stronghold in New York. Joining forces with another Connecticut son, Ethan Allen, they accomplished their mission.

In June, Congress asserted its constitutional authority by adopting "Articles of War" to govern the newly established Continental army. Connecticut's "Captain-General and Commander in Chief of the English Colony of Connecticut," Jonathan Trumbull, wasn't far behind. During Washington's call for reinforcement, he commissioned new state regiments to be sent in defense of New York City. East Haddam's Colonel Samuel Selden, serving under the command of General James Wadsworth, took his force into the Battle of Long Island. There, just after the American retreat, Selden was captured, taken prisoner and eventually died in a New York City prison.[20]

As the year closed, the United Colonies had a military force, relevant branches included—even if loosely defined. Four provinces had also come to the forefront. Acknowledged for their stature, experience and concern for individual rights would be Virginia, South Carolina,

The Colonel Samuel Selden Homestead, Selden's Neck, Hadlyme, Connecticut. *HABS CONN,6-HADLY,2—3.*

Massachusetts and Connecticut. When this vanguard pressed forward, the other colonies followed.[21]

Since so few battles were fought on Connecticut soil, casual observers are often surprised to learn that the colony's residents fought in nearly every early campaign. Residents were not only engaged, but in some cases, they also funded these actions—Ticonderoga, for one.[22] And if Connecticut support weren't enough by land, it also shined at sea and, as you will later learn, even below it. The state's maritime efforts ranged from successful privateering campaigns—providing near constant British harassment—to quality shipbuilding.[23]

Certainly, it was one thing to build frigates as imposing as the *Trumbull* and *Bourbon*, which Connecticut did, but to outfit them accordingly was equally grand. It took a special type of individual to endure a maritime mission. Imagine traveling east, when the average sailing time was four to six weeks to Great Britain. Westward, as expected, took even longer, usually six to eight weeks, routing and wind dependent.

THE LEBANON EPICENTER

With the outbreak of hostilities, Governor Jonathan Trumbull was forced to convert his family store in Lebanon into a "War Office." Resting just off the majestic town green, the small frame building would manage the war effort for eight straight years until 1783. More than 1,100 times between 1775 and 1783, he and his Council of Safety would meet to organize Connecticut's war effort.

Governor Trumbull's War Office, in Lebanon, Connecticut, became the headquarters for the defense of the colony. HABS *CONN,6-LEBA,2—1.*

An experienced mercantilist, Trumbull had transformed himself into an astute politician; that life began with his election to the Connecticut General Assembly in 1733 and continued for the next five decades. The efforts made by his Council of Safety to coordinate the supply of provisions—food, clothing and munitions—was most admirable; considering the lack of finances, raw materials and certain types of manufacturing, perhaps "miraculous" would be a better adjective.

Lebanon was the quintessence of the Connecticut cause; standing on the direct route to Boston, the town ranked fourteenth in population, eleventh in taxable property and third in the number of men who responded to the Lexington alarm. To the cause of freedom, Lebanon's allegiance was unparalleled.[24]

1776 AND BEYOND

Connecticut colonists, many awakened by the publication of Thomas Paine's *Common Sense*, proceeded to answer the call of a new year. Regiments continued to be promptly furnished by reenlistments and recruits, and supplies, especially gunpowder, were constantly monitored.

On July 12, 1776, four days after it was read in public, the news of the adoption of the Declaration of Independence was officially received by the state's Council of Safety. The governor's proclamation six days later states the matter succinctly, reporting that the coming campaign would "in all probability determine the fate of America."[25]

An example of Connecticut's support for the new commander in chief is this noteworthy interchange: On August 7, 1776, George Washington wrote to Trumbull that the British forces concentrating at New York had, by reliable accounts, reached 30,000, while the number of American soldiers fit for duty was 10,514 men, mostly raw troops scattered over a distance of some fifteen miles. A concerned Trumbull responded immediately by meeting with his Council of Safety "and ordered nine regiments of our militia, in addition to the five Western regiments, fourteen in the whole, to march without loss of time to join you." (These troops would be under the command of Oliver Wolcott, Esq.)[26] Trumbull also proposed volunteers (not in the militia) to march to Washington's assistance and even promised them like wages and allowance of provisions.[27] From accounts, it appears that twenty-one regiments of Connecticut militia were sent forward to New York, including the regiment of "Old Put."

An assessment by Washington in the spring of 1777 yields the obvious: the army must adopt a defensive strategy. He would fight a "War of Posts," also called a "Fabian strategy" after the Roman general Fabius Cunctator, to preserve precious resources. Withdrawing whenever his army was at risk was a shift in thinking for the leader, but it was an effective tactic; on the conventional battlefield, the Continental army could not compete with British regulars. This master plan would also include a greater dependency on espionage; he would gather intelligence, gauge its value and then select his battles—be them strategic or symbolic—and fight accordingly.[28]

As Connecticut resources adjusted to the new tactics, they would do so to their own detriment; the British occupation of New York City had always left the region vulnerable to attack. General Tryon, who had raided Danbury in 1777, turned his sights to New Haven, Fairfield and Norwalk in 1779. His goal of persecution without occupation proved a success. Later, turncoat Arnold's 1781 rampage of New London and Groton subjected colonists to unthinkable destruction. While significant British death preceded the colonist capitulation in New London, to witness the stabbing death of Colonel William Ledyard and the massacre of eighty surrendering Americans must have been horrific. With that insult not enough, Arnold also ordered New London burned.

Connecticut remained in a defensive mode for the remainder of the war. While most residents believed the British weren't willing to sacrifice New York for a Connecticut occupation, sleeping with one eye open was never easy.

OBSERVATION

The American Revolution, supported by the resources of the State of Connecticut, was the collaborative effort of thousands of dedicated Patriots—not just protagonists like John Adams, Thomas Jefferson and George Washington but also ordinary people—who took control of their political destiny. That was the "Spirit of '76," and it wasn't limited to a single year.

This attitude also manifested itself below the surface, where America's history of spying had begun. It would be the "spymaster" himself, George Washington, who declared its need when he said, "The necessity of procuring good intelligence is apparent." Covert operations, once viewed as insufferable, had now become acceptable. However, Washington did warn that the process depended on confidentiality, "for upon secrecy, success depends in most enterprises."

As America succeeded at divining British military maneuvers and at manufacturing misinformation, the enemy stood shaken yet stirred. Returning to England after the Revolutionary War, Major George Beckwith, London's spymaster in the colonies, bitterly remarked, "Washington did not really outfight the British; he simply outspied us!"

II. Spies Like Us

Chapter 2

The Spy

All knowledge that is divorced from justice must be called cunning.
—Plato, Greek philosopher

S pying existed centuries before the American Revolution: the ancient Egyptians had developed an intelligence system, the Greeks and Romans employed spies and feudal Japan used ninja to gather information. Although dynamic, the methodology of the spy was familiar to many by the time of the Seven Years' War. It was during this conflict that George Washington, serving under British general Edward Braddock, witnessed firsthand the life-changing value of intelligence.[29] He would later remark, "There is nothing more necessary than good intelligence to frustrate a designing enemy, and nothing that requires greater pains to obtain."[30]

Call them what you may, be it secret agents, intelligence agents, double and undercover agents, even moles, sleepers, plants or scouts; to most, they are simply spies. They collect and report information on the activities, movements and plans of an enemy.

Their role was simple: to know yet not be known. It was a discreet and clandestine function. Obscurity was paramount not only to the art but also to one's survival. Working for a government, organization or simply for themselves—greed never far from opportunity—success was measured not only in the maintenance of anonymity but also in the caliber of information gathered. Quality intelligence, as every spy understood, had an infinite demand during armed conflict. It was job security—if, of course, you could stay alive.

Second to none when it came to intelligence gathering, Washington understood that war changes people. *NPG–Smithsonian Institution, artist Gilbert Stuart.*

THE QUALITIES OF A SPY

As a vocation, what possesses an individual to pursue intelligence gathering ranges from patriotism in its purest form to out-and-out greed.[31] From the purity of Nathan Hale to the indignity of Benedict Arnold, in no place has this been better exemplified than in the state of Connecticut.

This forty-five-foot obelisk, known as the Captain Nathan Hale Monument, was erected in his honor in 1846. It is located inside the Nathan Hale Cemetery in Coventry, Connecticut.

Success, the proper delivery of the desired information, meant continued obscurity, while failure or high treason—the crime of betraying one's country—was punishable by death.

What made a good spy? While it is tempting to say that it was the New England air and Connecticut water, the truth was that it took much more. To this day, the foundation of successful intelligence gathering is not that far from what it was during the colonial period. Successful spies were handled with CAIR, an acronym for four distinguishing abilities: collection, assimilation, interaction and resolution.[32]

Collection: Attention to Detail

The ability to distinguish the relevant from the extraneous is why spying is often called intelligence gathering; a spy used for quartermaster duties needed to know the difference between feed and firearms. The process could require a level of analytical skills as well, such as math or geometry, perhaps even an extraordinary memory. Many of the spies who grace these pages had a strong academic prowess, which translated well to their art (Yale graduates, feel free to take a bow). Achievements in related professional skills, such as surveying (map construction) and mercantilism (trading), could also prove useful.

Assimilation: A Natural Fit

Often the biggest variable to a mission, assimilation was the ability to blend into the culture of choice without arousing suspicion. This familiarity included language (including dialect), clothing and mannerisms. For example, not every spy could survive in Boston's colonial maritime environment.

And even if you could speak, dress and act the part, that may not have been enough. Some missions called for a proficiency in certain skills, such as map reading, tracking or horseback riding. To look like a cavalry officer is one thing; to ride like one is another.

Interaction: Interpersonal Skills

Interpersonal skills are how people relate to one another—social interaction, if you will. Espionage frequently required a level of comfort with an entire spectrum of personality types, from farmer and merchant to deacon and administrator. For instance, gathering intelligence in the Cherokee lands of South Carolina, a spy was certain to come across a far different set of individuals than those walking the Post Road in Wethersfield, Connecticut. Agents understood that social acceptance was often directly proportionate to the quality of disclosed information.

Resolution: Self-sufficiency

Resolve, often the difference between life and death, was paramount to a spy. Overcoming the seemingly insurmountable mental and physical challenges must become commonplace; perfection, an acute mind combined with physical aptitude, was the ideal. From riding fifty miles in inclement weather to hunting for his next meal, an intelligence agent had to be self-reliant.

Self-sufficiency often meant an agent had to hunt, kill and then prepare his next meal. It could challenge a person's resolve, especially in inclement weather.

38

These four distinguishing abilities—collection, assimilation, interaction and resolution—had to be completed while keeping sentiments at a distance; the ability to dismiss emotions was needed to balance their acquisition. All these skills will surface in abundance in the chapters that follow.

AVAILABILITY AND PROCESS

Matching the distinct capabilities of a spy to a specific mission would have been ideal; however, there was no American Revolutionary Intelligence Academy or vast pool of candidates to choose from. Fertile ground would be those with army or militia experience or someone with similar skills to a mission's requirements. In truth, it was a challenging recruitment.

If enlistments were sparse, one might turn to the process itself. Using incentives, one might target someone close to the information. While an officer might be unlikely—propinquity to information of this nature often includes an insurmountable loyalty factor—looking down the chain of command for a weak link, someone involved with the process, such as an assistant, mapmaker or post rider, could be an option. As you can see, the art of eighteenth-century espionage wasn't that simple.

TECHNIQUES

Proficiency at spying techniques complemented an agent's aptitude. These techniques ranged from the simple, such as bribery and eavesdropping, to the complex, such as ciphering. Popular methods included clandestine meetings, code making (ciphering), counterespionage, dead drops, deception, diplomatic sleight of hand, disinformation, forgery, interrogation, networking, partisan warfare, propaganda, sabotage and scouting signals.

These practices were used to gain a tactical advantage. Since both sides of the conflict used intelligence, it often became a chess match. In 1775, when spies informed the British of munitions in Concord, they decided to take action and pursue the arsenal. In turn, that maneuver prompted colonial agents to inform their superiors and thus successfully counter the move. It was a classic "action/reaction" scenario, successful only because the information was immediately available.

Eavesdropping, or secret listening to a conversation, was as common as a Franklin witticism. A tavern room, such as the Leffingwell Inn, was the perfect environment. *HABS CONN,6-NORT,16—7.*

Washington loved using disinformation and deception. In 1781, he fooled the British, then occupying New York, into thinking that an assault was imminent. The move was successful because he tailored disinformation—from correspondence to simulated maneuverers—specifically to the weakness of his enemy. He then turned south toward Virginia and Yorktown.

Eavesdropping was as common as a Franklin witticism. Informants, often regional, provided much of the information gathered using this technique. Often this took place in a tavern or a relaxed place for social interaction. In Connecticut, it occurred in places like the Alden Tavern in Lebanon, the Asa Barnes Tavern in Southington or the Daniel White Tavern in Andover—locations that were also sites along the Washington-Rochambeau Revolutionary Route. Naturally, the imbibing of spirits may have added to loose tongues, but it took someone, be it a spy or informant, to be in the right place at the right time to utilize this information.

DECEPTIVE METHODS

Of the more fascinating deceptive techniques were inks, secret codes, templates and the manner in which information was transported. This is not to say that areas such as forgery are not interesting—just less common among those represented in this work. Copying included everything from watermarks and wax seals to various pens, inks and paper. A spy would often choose the technique he or she felt most comfortable with.

Inks

Benjamin Thompson, a well-known American scientist, did not believe in the Patriots' cause, nor did he intend to be quiet about it. As an avowed Loyalist, his actions ranged from returning British deserters to General Gage's headquarters in Boston—resulting in him being run out of his New Hampshire hometown—to discreet enemy correspondence using invisible ink.[33] Often a mix of ferrous sulfate and water, he would pen his secret message between the lines of an actual letter, thus encouraging the recipient to "read between the lines." Undetectable when written, these "sympathetic" inks appear—an effect that arises in response to an action—only when desired, thus the name.

Dating back to the third century BC, these inconspicuous inks, including milk, were written with a dip pen, such as a quill, and made visible by a special treatment, such as heat. Even lemon juice was used because the writing would not to appear until heat was applied. British agents used two methods for exposing their invisible ink: one through heat, the other through a chemical (acid) application. Later, Washington turned toward a more complex system using two solutions.

Secret Codes

Cryptography is the art of writing and solving codes, which are systems of words, letters, figures or symbols substituted for other words. It is a contradiction of sorts because it balances complexity with ease of use. As a technique used to secure communication in the presence of third-party adversaries, it is extremely effective. But it also requires a level of expertise to rearrange or change letters into different characters or symbols. That person, or cipher, accomplishes this task by using a key as a guide. A completed secret message will then have to be decrypted, using the same key, to be intelligible to the recipient. Without access to a key, the message would remain safe even if it fell into the hands of the enemy.

One rather simple technique involved character substitution, or having each letter of the alphabet replaced by a different letter, number or symbol. An often-cited example of this technique was an intercepted message sent by the gifted spy Dr. Benjamin Church to British General Gage. It revealed everything from provision levels and troop strength to a proposed attack on Canada. Complex as it may have been, it wasn't elaborate enough: the three ciphers selected to break the code for General Washington did it in a day or two. Test your code-breaking skills with the cryptograms (coded messages) that appear after the bibliography of this book.

America's first diplomatic cipher was Charles Dumas, a German scholar who befriended Benjamin Franklin and later John Adams; the former employed him as a secret agent. His system proved popular because it was easier than most and reliable—paramount for agents was choosing a system they felt comfortable with.[34]

James Lovell, often considered the "Father of American Cryptology," was a Harvard graduate and Continental congressman. His role as a member of the Committee of Foreign Affairs included writing and deciphering dispatches. While his cipher provided added security, it also confused his correspondents. This delicate balance was of utmost concern to a cryptologist.[35]

While minister to Spain from 1779 to 1782, John Jay used *Entick's Spelling Dictionary* to create a code rather than the popular page/column/word count method that could be applied to many popular books; these "dictionary codes" were extremely popular because all the words an agent might need were included inside.[36]

Code lists were also prevalent because users could create their own code by placing a number alongside a selected word. (See Chapter 12: "The Culper Ring.") Of course, this took time to develop, and subsequent copies, or keys, needed to be made for distribution. Even with these custom codes, there was no guarantee the cipher could not be broken.

But not having a key never stopped any adversary from using cryptanalysis, or the art or process of deciphering coded messages, to solve the mystery. "Black chambers," or secret offices used to examine correspondence sent by way of mail, have a long history in Europe and were often used successfully to foil espionage attempts.

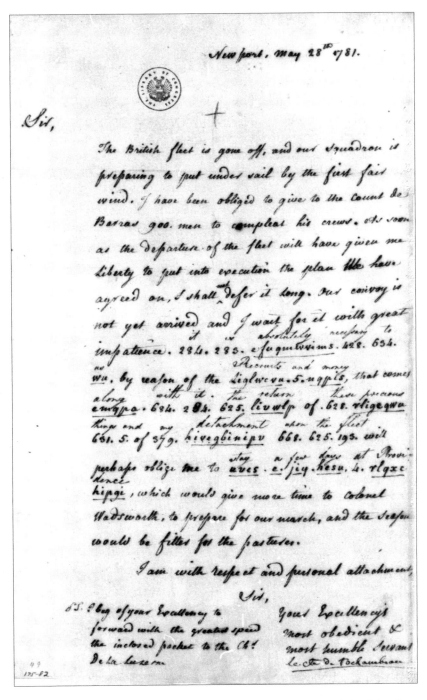

This letter from Rochambeau to Washington on May 28, 1781, included a cipher for security purposes. Note the words written above the Tallmadge code. *GWP-LC-S4.*

Templates

Concealing a message with a template was also used for security.[37] A mask is placed over a letter to reveal its true message; known as the Cardan System, it was named after sixteenth-century code maker Geronimo Cardano. The process begins by selecting a piece of paper—preferably that of a popular size—and then folding it in half. An arbitrary or selected shape is then cut into the paper and the piece removed. When the paper is opened up, you have your mask. An identically sized vellum is selected and placed under the template to reveal the hidden message area. Carefully, the intelligence agent will next write the desired message inside this mask. The template is set aside, and the agent then camouflages the message with additional writing; this is difficult, as the letter must make sense with or without the template. The mask will then be sent to the subject along one route, with the coded message along an alternate, to avoid interception.[38] This method was used successfully by the British.

Concealment/Hiding

Couriers on horseback, and even those on foot, transported information both written and verbal. Their goal was to reach journey's end safely and without interruption. Both armies would routinely stop strangers or riders and question them; often, this interrogation began with loyalty and destination. Obvious items, such as saddlebags of mail or unusual objects were commonly examined. This was followed by a visual examination; since messages could be hidden anywhere—inside books, buttons, hats, powder horns, shoes and quills—many items would be questioned.[39] This could be a taxing ordeal for the courier, never certain that he or she wouldn't be robbed, taken hostage or, God forbid, killed. It was an arduous task frequently disproportionate to the reward.

Washington, well aware of the British superiority when it came to spying, relied on everything from sympathetic civilians to mercenaries during the early days of the Revolution. Since British moles were as common as dysentery—and often equally as painful—he had little choice but to cautiously consider whatever form presented itself. In 1775, he began receiving some assistance from the Continental Congress, as committees (Correspondence, Secret and Spies) added a large-scale level to intelligence gathering. Their observations were not daily, but they processed activities such as Benjamin Franklin's covert acquisition of military aid. Franklin, masterful in most any action, parried with spies in France in 1776 like a talented London pugilist. It seemed that every wall in Paris had more than one ear against it.

WASHINGTON'S INTELLIGENCE PHILOSOPHY

On July 15, 1775, the eleventh entry into George Washington's expense account—or *Accounts, G. Washington with the United States, Commencing June 1775, and Ending June 1783, Comprehending a Space of 8 Years*—reads, "To 333⅓ Dollars given to [blank] to induce him to go into the Town of Boston, to establish a secret correspondence for the purpose of conveying intelligence of the Enemys movements and designs."[40] It is not the only such entry for the commander in chief of the Continental army, simply the first.

In his role, Washington became America's first director of military intelligence. His philosophy, he hoped, would be adopted by his subordinates. "It is a matter of great importance to have early and good intelligence of the Enemy's

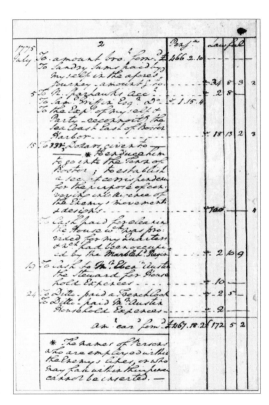

Inside Washington's expense account: "To 333⅓ Dollars given to [blank] to induce him to go into the Town of Boston, ... conveying intelligence." *LC-GW, Revolutionary War Expense Account.*

strength and motions as far as possible, designs and to obtain them through different channels," he would write.[41] As a hands-on information manager, he directed operations and performed his own analysis. It was through his effort that the army became proficient at espionage. (As is appropriate, we will never know the extent of his reconnaissance matrix because neither Washington nor his many sources ever revealed such information.)

But observations aren't always perfect, nor are they overt. Washington's September 11, 1777 attempt to thwart the British advance to Philadelphia at Brandywine was nearly a disaster. Outflanked but not outsmarted, he managed to get a spy network in place—thanks to Major John Clark—before British occupation.

By the spring of 1780, the British had begun the southern phase of the war with the conquest of Charleston, South Carolina. Meanwhile, Washington remained in New York, content with augmenting his intelligence network with the assistance of his Connecticut cohorts.

Chapter 3
A Call for Administration and Recruits

It does not take a majority to prevail...but rather an irate, tireless minority, keen on setting brushfires of freedom in the minds of men.
—*Samuel Adams,* The Writings of Samuel Adams, 1722–1803

Nearly every aspect of relations among Britain, France and Spain was altered by the French and Indian War. For the settlements of these European powers, this was a major consideration. Inside the thirteen British colonies located along the Atlantic seaboard, the overriding issues became security and individual rights. Groups began to emerge in colonial cities to answer these concerns. Some were established, like the Boston Caucus Club (circa 1719), led by political agitator and propagandist Samuel Adams, while others were born from consternation, such as the Sons of Liberty, which became the predominant voice. The latter's motto, "No taxation without representation," evolved into a battle cry against the abuses of the British government.

In late 1772, Adams, a second cousin to President John Adams, created new Committees of Correspondence to link all thirteen colonies. Composed of community leaders, this nationalist network grew swiftly as an effective conduit for information and disinformation. It was the leadership from these committees that controlled much of the American resistance to British actions, particularly at the local level.

This proliferation of patriotism also meant an increase in covert activities, much of it conducted by members of informal resistance. Early in the American Revolution, circa 1774, groups like the Sons of Liberty were superseded by more formal organizations such as the Committees of Safety, the benefit being that the local militias were usually under the control of the committees, which in turn sent representatives to county- or colony-level assemblies to represent their interests. By 1775, this had essentially become a provisional government—so much so that others, including the European powers, began to take notice.

A CONVICT IN CONNECTICUT: PROMPTING A SOLUTION

"I have now a painful tho' a Necessary Duty to perform respecting Doctor Church, Director General of the Hospital," wrote General George Washington. A future letter, dated October 5, 1775, was addressed to the president of the Continental Congress, John Jay, and it was to inform him that a hostile dispatch from Dr. Benjamin Church, surgeon general of the Continental army, had been intercepted. To everyone's astonishment, it had been sent to Lieutenant General Sir Thomas Gage, British commander in chief for North America. The Continental army had its first traitor![42]

The discovery had come about through a rather unusual routing. A coded letter to a British officer, Major Crane, had been carried by "a Woman who was kept by Doctor Church." The letter found its way to a friend of Nathanael Greene and then into the hands of Greene himself. When Washington received the letter from Greene, he had the women apprehended. After a lengthy interrogation, the inamorata admitted the identity of its author, Dr. Benjamin Church.

Washington was abashed, for it was he who, only months ago, had appointed Church. The renowned Boston physician, also a member of the Provincial Congress, a Harvard classmate of John Hancock and an outspoken Patriot, had been a two-faced traitor on the British payroll since 1772. The same man, who in his role as a local dignitary had escorted Washington into Cambridge, would now find himself ushered by guards and facing an army court-martial on October 4, 1775.

Although his decoded note contained a powerful statement of allegiance to the British Crown, Church, as expected, vehemently denied all allegations. He was tried, convicted and imprisoned for life—part of the latter included a stay in a Norwich, Connecticut gaol. Following an illness, Church was exiled. The ship he boarded, bound for the West Indies, was lost at sea.

Right: A diagram of the guardhouse and Simsbury mines, now called Old New-Gate Prison, and the "descent to Hell." *LC-USZ62-50390.*

Below: An outside view of Old New-Gate, a prison for the confinement of Loyalists in Connecticut and a place where death became a viable option. Some refer to it as Old Newgate Prison or simply Newgate.

On November 7, 1775, shortly after his conviction, the Continental Congress added a mandate for the death penalty as punishment for acts of espionage to the "articles of war." The entire incident struck fear in the hearts of New England residents, who now pondered how many other Benjamin Churches there might be. It also invited congressional action, such as the Committee of Spies.

For some, like the Tories—American colonists who supported the British side—sentenced to East Granby's Old Newgate Prison, the "descent to Hell," as some called it, was worse than death. A forty-foot ladder led straight down a main shaft to a dank and dismal cavern. Once a heavy iron grill capped this mineshaft, there was no way out. The former copper mine welcomed its first prisoner in 1773 and shut down in 1827.

Committee Work:
The Foundation of Modern Intelligence

During the first two years of the American Revolution, colonial governments coordinated their *formal* resistance to British rule through the Continental Congress (1774–81). For thirteen colonies that still recognized the British Crown, it was, as one might imagine, an extremely delicate process.

A nonthreatening but often effective form of organization was the creation of committees, albeit most with limited shelf lives. This group of individuals—appointed for a specific function and typically consisting of members of a larger group—was expected to better handle the concerns of the day, be they security issues or disciplinary actions.

Three committees laid the foundation for modern intelligence.

Secret Committee

Created on September 18, 1775, the covert agency employed agents overseas to gather intelligence and obtain military supplies. Those members of the Continental Congress chosen were Thomas Willing (Pennsylvania), Benjamin Franklin (Pennsylvania), John Dickinson (Pennsylvania), Philip Livingston (New York), John Alsop (New York), Thomas McKean (Delaware), John Langdon (New Hampshire), Samuel Ward (Rhode Island) and Silas Deane (Connecticut).

Committee of (Secret) Correspondence/ Committee for Foreign Affairs, 1775–77

The Second Continental Congress established the Committee of Correspondence (soon renamed the Committee of Secret Correspondence) on November 29, 1775. The need for quality foreign intelligence and improved worldwide alliances was the reason behind America's first foreign intelligence agency. On the committee were Benjamin Franklin, Benjamin Harrison and Thomas Johnson; they were soon joined by others, including James Lovell, the father of American cryptanalysis. As the need for diplomacy grew, so did the agency; it later changed its name to the Committee for Foreign Affairs. The committee employed secret agents abroad and conducted covert operations.

Committee on Spies

The Congress appointed a committee on June 5, 1776, to consider disciplinary measures against those charged with aiding the enemy; this arose through the capture of Dr. Benjamin Church. Members included John Adams, Thomas Jefferson, Robert Livingston, Edward Rutledge and James Wilson.

On August 21, 1776, the committee's report was considered by the Congress, which enacted the first espionage act:

> RESOLVED, That all persons...of the 29th of June last, who shall be found lurking as spies in or about the fortification or encampments of the armies of the United States, or of any of them, shall suffer death, according to the law and usage of nations, by sentence of a court martial, or such other punishment as such court martial may direct.

It was resolved further that the act "be printed at the end of the rules and articles of war."

With both formal and informal intelligence engaged, fulfilling the growing demand for spies became the issue. After all, without proper execution, even the ideal spying method could prove ineffective. Since CAIR—collection, assimilation, interaction and resolution—was the need, then perhaps a similar acronym could provide the solution. CAIR—"Connecticut Answers the Intelligence Required"—was not an immediate resolution, nor was it perfect, but it was a viable alternative from a state that prided itself on taking action.

A CONNECTICUT INTELLIGENCE DIRECTORY

A profusion of spies from the American Revolution—including British Commander Howe's dangerous liaisons, Moses Dunbar (Hartford), Robert Thomson (Newtown) and John Lyon (Fairfield County)—lived and worked in the colony of Connecticut.[43] Some even took orders from or labored alongside spies born here. Be it heritage, which is the assertion of this title, or coincidence, as some so casually claim, there was an undeniable comfort level with the task and the location.

While agents could vary in age, race, sex, national origin, religion, marital status, education, military experience and—as one might expect—proficiency in espionage, it was not, as you will witness, a rich diversity. The ultimate variable—allegiance—could also differ. With so many factors to consider, from past experiences and commitments to individual biases and economic factors, choosing sides wasn't always that simple.

To borrow a line from Keats, who was only four years old when Washington passed, "Nothing ever becomes real 'til it is experienced." As a preamble to a procession of the state's most famous scouts, meet a selection of eight lesser-known spies of Revolutionary Connecticut.

Dr. Samuel Adams

Born in 1730 in Stratford, Connecticut, Samuel Adams—not the Adams previously mentioned—became a physician and surgeon. In 1764, lured like so many others by the New Hampshire grants, he and his wife, Martha Curtis, along with their first five children, packed their belongings and headed to Arlington, Vermont. For years, they raised their family in this new settlement, slowly developing their property and even accumulating additional land.

Things went smoothly until the family clashed with Ethan Allen's Green Mountain Boys—not a surprise to those of you who have read ahead—over their land title policy. After a brief trial, Adams suffered a terrible public humiliation: he was tied to a chair and hung from a post. If that was not enough, two years later, he and his sons were imprisoned for his Loyalist sympathies.

Adams then escaped his captors and fled to Quebec. Joining the King's Army, he served during the Lake Champlain campaign in the autumn of 1776 and even raised his own independent Loyalist company, Adam's

Rangers, during the Burgoyne Expedition in 1777. The Rangers, many recruited from Vermont, ran successful reconnaissance missions and even defended Loyalist farms from Patriot foraging parties. He served alongside four of his sons and, following the war, settled among family in southeastern Ontario.

James Aitken

While in Paris, Silas Deane encountered James Aitken. Whether it was purely by chance or fate, the American agent engaged Aitken's services to sabotage the Royal Navy, even issuing him a passport signed by the French foreign minister, Charles Gravier, Comte de Vergennes.

Known under numerous monikers including "John the Painter," Aitken terrorized British naval dockyards from late 1776 until early 1777. After a lengthy manhunt, Aitken was finally captured in March 1777 and sent to the gallows on March 10, 1777. As a grim reminder about the consequences for such behavior, his decaying body was placed in a cage that was suspended for months at the British dockyard.[44]

Daniel Bissell

Author and historian Henry R. Stiles paints a picture of this Connecticut hero in *The History and Genealogies of Ancient Windsor, Connecticut (1635–1891), Vol. I* , saying, "And finally we had the extreme pleasure of vindicating the

Birthplace marker for Daniel Bissell, commemorating "a life of devotion to his country's interests, and of suffering in her service, such has been seldom paralleled."

deserter's character [Bissell], and of bringing to light the record of a life of devotion to his country's interests, and of suffering in her service, such has been seldom paralleled, even in the roll of brave deeds which ennoble the page of American History."[45]

Posing as a deserter in the city of New York from August 14, 1781, to September 29, 1782, Daniel Bissell was selected by General George Washington for a dangerous spying mission. Bissell, the eldest son of Daniel and Elizabeth (Loomis) Bissell of Windsor, was born on the family farm on December 30, 1754. By the time of his selection, he was seasoned, having served at White Plains, Trenton and Monmouth, with even a battle scar as proof.

Over three decades later, Bissell would recall his assignment in an affidavit: "Col. Heman Swift, of the 2nd Connecticut Regiment, called on me early in the morning [August 13, 1781], and stated to me that he dined at Head Quarters the day before, and His Excellency found it necessary to send within the British lines, to ascertain their position and force, some person, and that I was determined on for the undertaking." Bissell then confirmed receiving orders, which he read and then destroyed, from Colonel David Humphreys of Derby, Connecticut.

To the best of Bissell's recollection, his vigorous orders read, "As Gen. Arnold is now in Virginia, with all the new raised corps, there will be no recruiting parties in New York; and as the fleet is now at the Hook, consequently there will be no press [gang] in the city."[46] The impress service, commonly called a press gang, was employed to force someone to serve in an army or navy. To enter New York as a deserter, Bissell had three options: post rebel bail, pay seventy pounds or enlist in the British army. Bissell continued, "And with the money you carry in, you can get a protection from the Mayor or Police of the city, to go to Lloyd's Neck, thirty miles on Long Island, to cut wood for the Crown."

After this, Bissell was ordered to King's Bridge or Laurel Hill, with detailed observation orders, such as troop strength and number of cannons, before similar inspections on York Island, Manhattan; Powler's Hook, Jersey City, opposite New York City; Staten Island; and Sandy Hook. Bissell also conducted a "Harbour" evaluation prior to surveillance on Long Island. "When you get the business completed," Bissell recalled being told, "the seventh or ninth night, be at a place called Whitestone, not far from Lloyd's Neck, where a boat will attend to fetch you off. In case you cannot attend on one of those nights, you will then make your escape off at the east end of Long Island."

Bissell then recounted what he had observed:

But when I arrived in New York, to my great disappointment, I found that Gen. Arnold had returned and had established his recruiting parties in every place where deserters could come in; and that press-gangs were in every part of the city; that the Commander-in-chief Sir Henry Clinton, had issued a late order that there should be no more protections given to deserters. After avoiding the press-gang for three days, and being attacked with a violent fever, I caused my name to be enrolled in Arnold's regiment.[47]

Bissell enlisted to receive medical attention and was hospitalized; he could not complete his orders as instructed. Suffering under agonizing conditions—unable to walk and still dressed in apparel he had worn for months, he was covered head and body with lice—the weeks quickly turned to months. "In this situation, I was taken out of the hospital to do Quarter-Master Sergeant's duty, for said regiment, by Capt. Robert Rowley," he would recall.[48]

Although Bissell did not account for his escape in his affidavit, it proved, by most accounts, nothing short of dramatic.[49] From crossing rivers and swamps with a companion who could not swim to even being chased by a British light horse, the spy endured overwhelming odds.

Upon his successful return to the American lines, Bissell spent two days writing a descriptive account of his nearly thirteen-month ordeal, his thought being that it would be worthy of recompense. But reward for his efforts would not be forthcoming; during his duration, Congress had ordered there be no more commissions given. Faced with a number of options, including a discharge, he returned to his regiment and did orderly sergeant duty until May following.

The third person to receive the Badge of Military Merit (Purple Heart) during the Revolutionary War, Bissell was preceded by two other Connecticut natives: Sergeant William Brown, Fifth Connecticut Regiment of the Connecticut Line, and Sergeant Elijah Churchill, Second Connecticut Light Dragoons.[50]

John Clark

Operating in and around Philadelphia during the British occupation, John Clark conducted one of the most successful spy rings of the American Revolution. Although gifted in the art of networking, it was his reconnaissance work on Long Island that first drew the attention of George Washington. He eventually became a trusted confidant of the commander in chief. While he is best remembered—

and well he should be—for his masterful deception against General Howe, Clark did manage some very successful operatives, including his Connecticut contact, Benjamin Tallmadge.[51] (See Chapter 12: "The Culper Ring.")

William Heron

A Native of Cork, Ireland, William Heron found his way to Redding, Connecticut, just before the Revolution. There, in 1772, he bought the home of Anglican reverend John Beach. A publication entitled *Sir Henry Clinton's Secret Service Record of Private Daily Intelligence*, which surfaced in 1882, revealed that teacher and surveyor William Heron, aka Hiram the Spy, was a self-serving double agent.

This was a surprise, considering that Heron was active on numerous committees while serving in the Connecticut General Assembly and was even provided with passes that allowed him travel access to New York by Governor Trumbull. An unsuspecting General Samuel Holden Parsons of Lyme, Connecticut, also gave his personal approval of the man—the personal dynamics between Heron and Holden could be a book in itself—in a letter to George Washington dated April 6, 1782. Heron was also believed to be the source of enemy speculation regarding the Culper Ring.

Solomon Johns

Solomon Johns became a British Revolutionary War hero. Born on February 24, 1751, in Litchfield County, Connecticut, both he and his father, Benjamin, got caught up in the excitement of the New Hampshire grants. The thought of a healthy parcel of land in Vermont attracted many New Englanders. Johns married Susanna Bucklin in 1775; it is believed they settled on their Vermont stake.

As the Revolution took form, Johns took sides. When safety concerns caused the family to leave their homestead, the State of Vermont confiscated the property in 1778; it was seizing vacated property to raise state revenue. It was then that Johns turned north and became part of the King's Rangers, or "Rogers Rangers," as they were also called, headquartered at Fort St. Johns (now St. Jean) in Quebec, Canada. The group became known for its covert activities; it is believed Johns was captured and incarcerated in a Vermont prison for aiding the enemy and later exchanged. Johns continued to serve with the King's Rangers until the war ended.[52]

Nehemiah Marks

Born on October 9, 1746, in Derby, Connecticut, Nehemiah Marks was the son of a successful merchant. In 1770, he married Elizabeth Hawkins, also of Derby; the couple is believed to have had eight children. Along with a conversion of faith—he was a Shepardic Jew who converted to the Anglican faith—Marks also underwent a transformation of loyalty. After the Revolution began, he went to New York City, where he acted as a British agent. Making frequent clandestine crossings between Long Island and Connecticut, he was the British version of Caleb Brewster (see Chapter 12: "The Culper Ring"). Speaking of Brewster, both Marks and Heron were aware of his frequent travels across Long Island Sound. Following the evacuation of New York City, he sought refuge in Canada.[53]

Noah Phelps

On the afternoon of April 30, 1775—less than a week after Ethan Allen learned of the slaughter at Lexington and Concord—three riders approached the unofficial capitol of pre-Revolutionary Vermont, the Catamount Tavern. Heman Allen, brother of Ethan and himself a prominent figure in the early history of the state, had ridden all night alongside Captains Edward Mott and Noah Phelps, both French and Indian War veterans. They brought with them orders from Hartford stating that the now colonel, Ethan Allen, in command of the Green Mountain Boys, was to attack the Lake Champlain forts of Ticonderoga and Amherst, acquire cannons and move hastily toward Boston. To accept Connecticut's commission—an attack on the monarch's forts—was a blatant act of treason punishable by a traitor's death. But to be enslaved by Great Britain, as Allen thought, was simply not an alternative.

Noah Phelps, born on January 22, 1740, to David and Abigail Pettibone Phelps, was the fourth of nine children. Phelps married Lydia Griswold of Windsor, Connecticut, on June 10, 1761. The couple settled in Simsbury, the site of their wedding, and looked after a large family. As a prominent town member, Phelps was commissioned a lieutenant in the militia in 1771, captain in 1774, lieutenant colonel in 1777, brigadier general in 1792 and major general in 1796.[54]

Ethan Allen dispatched both Phelps and Ezra Hickok to play the role of unkempt fur traders in order to gain access to Fort Ticonderoga.[55] While it may sound a bit crazy now, it was not out of the ordinary for the

The Strong family burial plot in Bolton, Connecticut, includes Noah Phelp's stepfather Deacon David Strong and his mother, Abigail (Pettibone) Phelps Strong.

time—Allen had witnessed the condition before. Once inside, the pair made an immediate switch to observation, noting sentinels' positions and fort conditions. The mission yielded a treasure-trove of information: the gunpowder supply had been damaged, the gates to Ticonderoga were left open because the keys had been lost, the British garrison included forty-six regulars and two officers and the arrival of reinforcements was imminent.[56] The following evening, the company captured the fort without a single loss. The reconnaissance operation was an unmitigated success.

Upon his return to Simsbury, Phelps remained active in the community; he chaired the town meeting that passed the Articles of Confederation in January 1778, and in November 1787, the town picked him and Daniel Humphreys as delegates for the convention of the state of Connecticut.[57]

Over the years, the state of Connecticut has garnered a few nicknames, including the "Provisions State." Since provision is the action of providing or supplying something for use, then what better than intelligence? Certainly, the state provided more than its fair share of victuals, but information, like supplies, saved lives. These awe-inspiring accounts are support for Connecticut's claim to an additional moniker, the "Intelligence State."[58] A bold but firm assertion, it need not reference the obvious, such as the thirty-two men who served as General George Washington's aides-de-camp, all of whom were involved in covert activities and three of whom bear direct state ties: David Humphreys, John Trumbull and Jonathan Trumbull Jr. It need only the endorsements that will follow in both Part III and Part IV.

III. Connecticut's Spies of the Revolution

Chapter 4

Silas Deane

Resentment is a passion, implanted by nature for the preservation of the individual. Injury is the object which excites it...A man may have the faculty of concealing his resentment, or suppressing it, but he must and ought to feel it. Nay he ought to indulge in it, to cultivate it. It is a duty.
—*John Adams, appointed a commissioner to France, to replace a man whom he had help appoint, "brother" Silas Deane*

As a secret envoy, Silas Deane had posed in the character of a merchant during a successful mission. Recalled to report on "the state of affairs in Europe," according to his instructions, Congress had "appointed another commissioner to supply his place there."[59] As a parasite of the soul, indignation can erode a man's values, even his patriotism. From this day forward, Silas Deane would die a slow and very painful death.

A WETHERSFIELD LOYALIST

Born in New London County, Connecticut, on Christmas Eve 1737, Silas Deane was the son of a land speculator and part-time farrier, also named Silas Deane. Taking little interest in ironworks or his father's other avocations, young Silas opted to study law. Graduating from Yale in 1758, Deane passed the bar in April 1761; ironically, while in study, one of the students he tutored

Left: A portrait from life of Silas Deane. *LC-USZ62-26779.*

Below: The historic home of Silas Deane in Wethersfield, Connecticut.

was Edward Bancroft, later doctor turned British agent who would serve as secretary to the American Commission in Paris.

As a young man, Deane chose Wethersfield—founded in 1634, it is located a few miles south of Hartford on the Connecticut River—as the center of both his legal and mercantile pursuits. He would also become an active West Indian trader.

Aggressive since birth, or so it seemed, Deane was perceptive, astute and hardworking. He courted the wealthy widow of Mr. Joseph Webb,

Mehitabel, five years his senior and mother of six.[60] There was much to be said of the pair, who were married on October 8, 1763; Deane, a handsome and well-mannered gentleman, would also assume the responsibility for a large family and thriving dry goods business.

Ambition often breeds challenge, and Deane had plenty of both. Not long after building a large and elegant home just north of his business in 1764, the birth of the couple's only child, Jesse, occurred that same year. This happiness was fleeting, however, as Mehitabel Nott Deane died on October 13, 1767. Following a period of mourning, Deane again sought companionship and found it in the charm of another widow: Elizabeth Saltonstall Evards, the daughter of a wealthy shipping merchant and granddaughter of an early Connecticut governor. Her husband had been lost at sea. Evards, similar to the first Mrs. Deane, also suffered health problems and passed away in 1777. Silas would learn of her death while serving in France.

POLITICAL POSTULATION

Wealth and opportunity stirred Deane's entry into the world of politics. He took a seat in the General Assembly in 1772 and two years later was sent to the First Continental Congress in August 1774. The latter appointment was attributable to Deane's efficiency as a member of the Committee of Correspondence, the creative financiers of Ticonderoga. Serving alongside Judge Roger Sherman of New Haven and Judge Eliphalet Dyer of Windham, Deane became a prolific and proficient congressional committee member.

When the Second Continental Congress was called in the spring of 1775, the trio was reappointed. But hostility grew between Deane and fellow Connecticut representative Roger Sherman; by fall, delegates to the Continental Congress were elected rather than appointed, and Sherman's organization defeated him. Politics, by nature, is dynamic, and the event, as strange as it may sound, marked a period of self-examination for Deane. Despite often-harsh criticism, he felt he had done justice to the appointment.

Instead of returning to Wethersfield, Deane stayed in Philadelphia, his hope being to assist the several committees he served, including the Committee of Secrecy.[61] His intuition, in this instance, proved correct.

As Agent

The astute vision of John Adams had foreseen the need for military supplies from Europe, a shared observation not fully supported until November 1775 with the appointment by Congress of the Committee of Secret Correspondence. It would be through this group, composed of some of the most eminent and trusted fathers of the Revolution, that critical international contacts were to be made; naturally, France, a rival and enemy of Great Britain, would be an obvious choice. When it became clear, and it didn't take long, that someone needed to personally appraise the French disposition—should the colonies decide to declare independence—the acute individual of choice was Silas Deane. His capabilities met the primary objective; should a treaty of alliance also find itself a part of the delicate mix, then so be it.

Appointed as a secret envoy to France on March 2, 1776, Deane's role was a combination of merchant, appraiser and intelligence officer, a clandestine capacity based on the *authority* of a Congress of thirteen united colonies still flying a "Union flag." Besides his official duties, Deane had private business assignments. As a probable scenario, it was a secure cover.

Setting sail on March 16, 1776, Silas Deane did not arrive in Bordeaux, France, until May.[62] Upon his arrival in Paris, he began executing his orders, a task he accomplished surprisingly well considering his unfamiliarity with the language and customs. His detailed instructions included letters of introduction, names of specific individuals to greet and even how to behave during the encounter. It was an awkward yet systematic circumstance.

As special agent, he was to buy supplies for Congress with money or credit from the sale of American commodities in Europe. His extensive list began with clothing and arms for twenty-five thousand men, ammunition and one hundred field pieces and articles for trade—linens and woolens—with the Indians. That this merchandise saw safe transatlantic passage was a given. Before the implausibility overwhelms you, let me affix some further details. Deane, patently bereft of savoir faire, had only a pocket filled with pounds (believed to be 200,000 Continental dollars) and promises. There seemed a peculiar cruelty associated with all this.

Patriotism—and an adjunct commission of 5 percent—provided the incentive. Complicating the mission was its timing: he was leaving behind a spouse of frail health, a young son and a somewhat tarnished reputation. On balance, it was the most delicate of all scenarios.

THE FRENCH PIPELINE

The situation in Paris was so complex that even Deane would never fully comprehend it. By the time Deane arrived, clandestine French aid to the Patriots was already in progress. His daily challenges alone were exasperating: his letters home went unanswered, he was running low on funding—and invisible ink, for that matter—and he was under constant surveillance by intelligence agents. He wrote to the Committee of Correspondence, "My arrival here, my name, my lodgings, and many other particulars have been reported to the British Administration."[63] Paris was irrefutably swarming with spies, most watching Deane or one another.

By July, it had become evident that the French would not violate the explicit terms of the 1763 treaty ending the Seven Years' War with Britain, a position affirmed by French foreign minister Comte de Vergennes. But Vergennes did suggest the use of private firms, in particular that of Roderiquez, Hortalez and Company (et Cie), a trading operation used as cover for secret French aid run by one Pierre-Augustin Caron de Beaumarchais.[64] Following a letter of introduction, Deane would meet Beaumarchais.

A view of the restored Golden Gates of Versailles in France. The Treaty of Paris was signed on September 3, 1783, at Versailles, close to the palace in the nearby foreign affairs building.

A flamboyant playwright best known for his works *Le Barbier de Séville, Le Mariage de Figaro, La Mère Coupable-Pierre*, Augustin Caron de Beaumarchais dabbled in everything from watchmaking to arms dealing; as a crafty schemer, the eclectic magnate had no parallel. For the French, he was an established secret agent and the ideal buffer. Let the chess match begin!

Working with Beaumarchais and other French merchants to procure ships, commission privateers and purchase military supplies, Deane managed to augment the Franco-American relationship. It was, however, Beaumarchais who convinced the special agent that as ordnance goes, so must officers; capable artillerymen must accompany these potentially dangerous weapons. So they did, through Deane's commissions. Although he had no authority to grant such assignments—a context that would eventually haunt him—he also had nobody to stop him.

In the fall of 1776, in a move to improve efficiency, Congress created an American Commission in Paris to supersede its individual agent; Deane would be named commissioner along with Benjamin Franklin and Arthur Lee.[65] Unfortunately, this created an entirely new set of dynamics that did little to improve communication.

By March 1777, Franklin had learned of Washington's December successes at Trenton and Princeton. Modest as they may have been, they signaled vulnerability. The inherent polymath, conscious that Versailles would not engage until a firm American victory had been had, now had his first step toward that objective. It was also a small tribute to French aid, as Washington's men had used some equipment supplied by Beaumarchais.

When the news of Burgoyne's surrender at Saratoga reached France, King Louis XVI decided to enter formal negotiations with the Americans. The treaty of alliance was signed on February 6, 1778.

ARTHUR LEE

Deane's appointment had crushed a covert plan that Arthur Lee had formulated in November 1775 with Beaumarchais.[66] The pair, with virtually no authority, had met in London to establish a lucrative arms deal. With two powerful brothers in Congress, Richard Henry and Francis Lightfoot, both of whom would have benefited from their brother's efforts, Arthur Lee had no intention of standing in any man's shadow and certainly not that of a Connecticut counselor; combining family influence with Deane's existing enemies in Congress, Lee believed, would ascertain the agent's recall and reinvigorate his long-term plan.

A University of Edinburgh–educated doctor and lawyer, Arthur Lee's behavior was a bit too sanctimonious and bilious for most. Silas Deane would pen, "From the first Mr. Lee gave Dr. Franklin and me much trouble which was constantly increasing; and the dissatisfaction with and contempt for the French nation in general, which he took no pains to conceal, often gave us pain, and rendered himself suspected by many."

Despite Deane's concerns, Lee would stay in Paris. Charged with embezzling funds that Congress had entrusted him to pay for supplies, Deane would be recalled and the victories at Trenton, Princeton and Saratoga, made possible by French provisions, conveniently overlooked. In 1779, Franklin was appointed sole minister plenipotentiary, and Lee was called back.[67]

THE RECALL

On March 4, 1778, Silas Deane received a letter from James Lovell. It was the order of Congress of December 8, 1777, requesting him to return home to report on the condition of affairs in Europe. On the advice of Franklin, Deane sailed with distinction aboard Charles D'Estaing's flagship, accompanied by Conrad A. Gerard (Gerard de Rayneval), the first French minister to the United States.

Deane's grand exit was in great contrast to his return to Philadelphia.[68] There he would engage his adversaries, most notably Thomas Paine, for well over a year, all in an attempt to defend himself against a body of unsubstantiated accusations, a controversy that would later fill nearly five hundred pages of the New York Historical Society's *The Silas Deane Papers* (1778–79). Having used his own assets for government business, he grew increasingly concerned about repayment.

In frustration, Deane went public with a statement on January 11, 1779. It was published in the *Pennsylvania Packet* three days later. In it, he defended himself against all congressional accusations. Paramount was the false assertion by Congress that the supplies provided were a present and not a commercial concern. Deane assured the public that it was a transaction and then listed the eight ships that sailed from France with the supplies.

Suffice it to say that Deane's proclamation did not sit well with the legislative body. Having seen and heard enough, Congress offered him $10,000 in

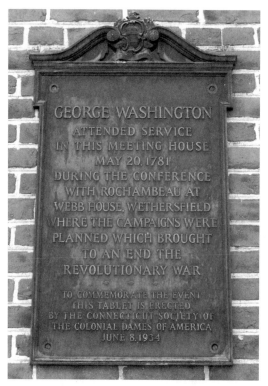

GEORGE WASHINGTON
ATTENDED SERVICE
IN THIS MEETING HOUSE
MAY 20. 1781
DURING THE CONFERENCE
WITH ROCHAMBEAU AT
WEBB HOUSE, WETHERSFIELD
WHERE THE CAMPAIGNS WERE
PLANNED WHICH BROUGHT
TO AN END THE
REVOLUTIONARY WAR

TO COMMEMORATE THE EVENT
THIS TABLET IS ERECTED
BY THE CONNECTICUT SOCIETY OF
THE COLONIAL DAMES OF AMERICA
JUNE 8.1934

Attached to the Wethersfield meeting house, just yards from the Deane home, rests this historic plaque.

depreciated currency. Deane refused. In March 1780, he then headed back to France to collect the vouchers needed to document some of his claims—as if the French would leave such incriminating documentation lingering about. There, it was hoped the matter would be finally closed; Congress had appointed Thomas Barclay, the consul at Paris, to review the materials. But it wasn't.

As Deane's health and finances failed, he assumed a transient lifestyle, an almost self-imposed exile. He moved to Ghent, Belgium, and then to England, even taking up with Dr. Edward Bancroft, whose role as a double agent for the British would not be revealed until about 1870. The inaction by Congress, a body that never levied any charges against him, essentially destroyed his spirit.

Despondent, Deane filled his time with defensive correspondence. Unfortunately, some of these letters were intercepted by British spies and published in the *Royal Gazette*, a New York Tory newspaper run by James Rivington; the provocation could be heard all the way to Wethersfield.[69] And there would be more. Published in 1784 was a pamphlet he penned entitled *To the Free and Independent Citizens of the United States of North-America*.[70] Inside, Deanne advocated that the colonies reconnect with England. In the hearts of his fellow countrymen, this was treason.

When Deane finally felt he could safely return to America on September 23, 1789, he boarded a ship at Deal in Kent. However, once aboard, Deane suffered a violent abdominal attack that caused paralysis and death; the lack of information surrounding his departure and mysterious passing has led to incessant speculation. His interment was believed to have been in the St. George's Churchyard in Deal.

LEGACY

During the time Silas Deane was appointed as a secret envoy to France, Oliver Wolcott, a fellow Connecticut delegate, assessed the moment as a point that could "decide the fate of the country." Of certainty is that France made funds and material available and that Silas Deane did receive vital supplies necessary to sustain the American armies during the demanding 1777 campaigns, including the essential victory at Saratoga; he also successfully recruited Lafayette, von Steuben, Pulaski and De Kalb.

Silas Deane's granddaughter and only heir, Philura Deane Alden, and her husband, Horatio Alden of Hartford, prepared a Memorial to Congress in 1835. It documented Silas Deane's claims for money owed him by the government; it was believed to have been a powerful statement. However, it took seven years before both houses awarded the heirs $37,000, a partial restitution, and described the original audit by a congressional committee under the chairmanship of his old enemy Arthur Lee as "ex parte, erroneous and a gross injustice to Silas Deane."

Suspicions of poisoning by Dr. Bancroft, an authority on toxins, have been revisited for years but remain unproven.

From frigates to freeways, Deane's name has adorned an assortment of things in the state of Connecticut. The Webb-Deane-Stevens Museum of Wethersfield is particularly noteworthy for its numerous restorations and continued education on the life and times of Silas Deane. Numerous resources, including websites such as Silas Deane Online, continue to offer a fascinating view of the Patriot.

Chapter 5

Ethan Allen

The Gods of the valley are not the gods of the hills, and you shall understand it.
—Ethan Allen, in response to the king's attorney-general decision against him in
a June 1770 New York court case[71]

From the colony of Connecticut came the call: a private directive to Ethan Allen to raise the Green Mountain Boys—an experienced militia group founded in the 1760s—and lead a surprise attack on Fort Ticonderoga. Allen, with his unbridled passion for life and liberty, was the embodiment of patriotism, an unrivaled choice for such a mission. Assisted by his brother Ira and their cousins Seth Warner and Remember Baker, the truculent leader accepted the challenge.

"FORT TI" VIA BENNINGTON

Composed of settlers and land speculators—many of whom held New Hampshire titles to land between the Connecticut River and Lake Champlain—Allen's militia were proficient frontiersmen and hardened infantry. When the forced march of 230 members began from Bennington, Vermont, a place "the Boys" called home, there was no consternation.[72] Arriving at their Champlain staging area on May 9, 1775, they prepared for battle.

At the junction of two waterways, Ticonderoga, New York, rests on the west side of Lake Champlain and at the north end of Lake George, twelve miles south of Crown Point and ninety-five north of Albany. The famous fortress, built by the French in the mid-eighteenth century, is situated at a narrows near the south end of the lake. It is an ideal location: defended on three sides by water and surrounded by rocks, and where that fails, the French erected a nine-foot-high breastwork. Without inhibition, Allen was certain to add his name to its distinguished provenance.

As a light mist began to fall during the afternoon, Allen addressed his men:

Friends and fellow soldiers, you have, for a number of years past been a scourge and terror of arbitrary power. Your valor has been famed abroad, and acknowledged, as appears by the advice and orders to me, from the General Assembly of Connecticut, to surprise and take the garrison before us. I now propose to advance before you, and, in person, conduct you through the wicket-gate; for we must this morning either quit our pretensions to valor, or possess ourselves of this fortress in a few minutes; and, inasmuch as it is a desperate attempt, which none but the bravest of men dare undertake, I do not urge it on any contrary to his will. You that will undertake voluntarily, poise your firelocks.[73]

Vermont monument marking the former site of the Catamount Tavern, home to Ethan Allen's Green Mountain Boys.

Dampening troops but not spirits, a storm had delayed the arrival of boats to cross the lake. Landing eighty-three men near the garrison before sending the boats back for his rear guard, Allen realized he was running out of time. As the morning of May 10 began to dawn, the experienced commander made the decision to attack. Having undergone his prerequisite reconnaissance (see Noah Phelps), he was fully aware of the dangers that lie ahead, and he drew up three ranks.

Performing as instructed, the men marched to the wicket. With the majority of the garrison asleep, "the Boys" met with little resistance. Led to a pair of stairs in front of a barrack, Allen ordered the commander, Captain De la Place, to come forth instantly or he would sacrifice the garrison. The captain complied. Standing in the door, breeches in hand, he demanded by what authority. Allen proclaimed, "In the name of the great Jehovah, and the Continental Congress" (likely not the perfect choice of words, but nevertheless effective).[74] Before the captain could question the declaration, Allen halted him. The spirited commander drew a sword over his head and again demanded an immediate surrender. Captain De la Place then capitulated.[75] Without a shot being fired, Ticonderoga—the Canadian gateway—had a new owner.

The captured armaments—about one hundred pieces of cannons, one thirteen-inch mortar and a number of swivels—were supplemented by ninety gallons of rum. While it was clear what to do with the arms, and the rum for that matter, the Green Mountain Boys had also to contend with prisoners, who were later presented to the Connecticut governor. When Colonel Warner arrived with the second wave, he was sent to take possession of Crown Point, which was garrisoned with only thirteen men. Also successful, Warner returned with a robust arsenal. The last remaining element was taking possession of a sloop lying at St. John's. This was accomplished under General Benedict Arnold—an unexpected arrival on May 9—who sailed north to raid Fort St. John and seize the sloop HMS *Royal George*.

A CONNECTICUT FOUNDATION

When Ethan Allen's grandfather Samuel died in 1718, the family responsibilities fell to Mercy Wright Allen, a very strong and determined woman. As a youth, Ethan would often hear stories about how his grandmother took her turn, alongside men twice her size, building the town fort. It was Mercy who decided to buy a proprietor's share in the new town of Litchfield, the latest frontier in the Berkshire foothills. Without her husband, she quickly put her six children to work tending to a new family farm. The town gradually became a prosperous Puritan community and an epicenter for trade in northwestern Connecticut. To the Allen family, it was finally, or so they thought, home.

When Mercy Allen died, one-third of her estate came into the hands of her youngest son, Joseph. Mature for his age, the nineteen-year-old was

The birthplace of Ethan Allen in historic Litchfield, Connecticut.

conservative by nature and steadfast in his religious beliefs. At the age of twenty-seven, Joseph married Mary Baker, and the couple settled on a seventy-two-acre farm one mile south of the Litchfield meetinghouse. One of eight children, Ethan Allen was born on January 10, 1737.[76] Following his religious convictions, Ethan's father then uprooted the family to a newly surveyed township twenty miles to the northwest of Litchfield. Located on the east bank of the Housatonic River, Cornwall would now be called home.

Proficiency in hunting and fishing came easy to Ethan, and later it would be complemented by an interest in philosophy. Like most living in the area, his education was informal, his inspiration drawn from his religious beliefs. His intellectual growth seemed to parallel that of his physical stature; he had grown to over six feet tall and was rather muscular. Of those who knew him, most would agree that he was destined to become a leader.

Ethan, with hopes of one day being admitted to Yale, had begun studying under a minister in Salisbury, but his father's death in 1755 forced him to abandon his efforts. His focus then shifted to family. Although he would volunteer for militia service in 1757, most of his emphasis was at home, on the farm or with a local love interest.

In July 1762, Ethan married Mary Brownson, and the couple settled in Cornwall. The following year, they moved to Salisbury, where Ethan had a stake in an ironworks. After he sold his interest in October 1765, he became self-absorbed and his behavior erratic.

In the spring of 1770, Allen, now in Bennington, made his first foray into Vermont land speculation; since this required travel, perhaps it contributed to his habitual disappearance. Mary's death in 1783 ended what many believed was a turbulent marriage; of their five children together, only two would reach adulthood. Allen then married Francis B. Montresor on February 9, 1784, in Westminster, Vermont.

Land Grants and Green Mountains

The flaw in the "get rich quick" New Hampshire Grants was that interested parties couldn't get or give clear title to the land. It was a clash between colonial governments, all claiming rights to present-day Vermont. In 1770, a group of grant holders asked Allen to get legally involved, which he did for the sake of his friends, family and himself. The outcome of a New York trial to determine the validity of the landholdings would not favor Allen's party.

When the group returned to Bennington, the settlers met at the Catamount Tavern to discuss their options. It was determined that any attempt made by the New York provincial government—Allen's confrontations with New York's governor William Tryon would become legendary—to establish its authority would be thwarted. Thus the formation of the Green Mountain Boys, led by the "Robin Hood of Vermont."

Following the favorable outcome at Ticonderoga and his aggressive yet convincing enforcement of land claims, it became clear that Ethan's ego could no longer fit inside the Catamount; he was voted out as commander of the Green Mountain Boys before they were incorporated into the Continental army.

Allen then pursued an ill-fated attempt to invade Canada and in September 1775 was captured by the British in Montreal. The account of his captivity is an engrossing read. Exchanged for a captured British officer in 1778, he returned to the colonies and reported to George Washington at Valley Forge, Pennsylvania. Allen didn't see action there, however, and returned to Vermont, where he became major general of the militia and went back to fighting territorial disputes.

U.S. senators honor the 200th anniversary of the birth of Ethan Allen by placing a wreath at his statue in Statuary Hall, Washington, D.C. *LC-DIG-hec-21976.*

Ethan Allen died on February 12, 1789, from what most believe to be an apoplectic fit. Burial came four days later in the Green Mountain (Greenmount) Cemetery in Burlington (Chittenden County), Vermont.

Afterword

A true Patriot, Ethan Allen was as obstinate as he was determined, as egotistical as he was loyal. As a friend, he had no rival.

When the British released Allen in 1778, likely as much of a relief to them as to Ethan, he returned home to a hero's welcome. Quickly settling near present-day Burlington in 1779, he couldn't resist the temptation to pen his manifesto, thus the publication of *A Narrative of Colonel Ethan Allen's Captivity*. It was not only a heroic adventure but a bestseller as well. Nothing would do more to solidify his legacy: Allen was now the prototypical Revolutionary leader, the hero of Vermont and an untamed product of the Green Mountains.

At the pinnacle of popularity, he pressed onward. Unsuccessful at petitioning Congress for its recognition of Vermont as an independent republic in 1777, he then spent three years negotiating with Great Britain to make the land a Crown province, the latter resulting in Congress charging Allen with treason. Proof of the old Vermont adage that you never go out on the ice unless you know how thick it is!

In 1785, when the halo began to fade, Allen published a second book, *Reason: The Only Oracle of Man*, which attacked Christianity. It was a complete failure. He then turned back to his family, farming and, of course, himself.

One of the Patriot's critics was Yale contrarian Timothy Dwight, who, upon Allen's death, penned that the world no longer had to deal with a man of "peremptoriness and effrontery, rudeness and ribaldry."

Chapter 6

Thomas Knowlton

*I doubt the state has produced a greater military genius or a more unselfish
patriot. The official recognition of his services and his great qualities comes late,
but his fame is permanent and it will increase, for it is the sort of heroism that the
people take to heart long after the flags are folded and the drums are silent.
—Charles Dudley Warner, November 13, 1895*[77]

T hey gathered, friends and
neighbors, around the winter
firesides of Windham County in
hopes that Thomas Knowlton, who
had enlisted as a private in the French
and Indian War, might share a tale or
two. The teenager, who had forged
his skills early in life as a woodsman,
had recently refined his aptitude with
military expertise. Under the guidance
of many an able officer, including

"I doubt the state has produced a greater
military genius or a more unselfish patriot,"
were the words Charles Warner used in 1895
to describe Thomas Knowlton.

Israel Putnam, and in multiple campaigns, such as the bloody Battle of Wood Creek (1758) and the Siege of Havana (1762), Knowlton excelled.

Ashford's Answer

Born on November 22, 1740, in West Boxford, Massachusetts, Thomas Knowlton's family relocated to Ashford, Connecticut, when he was eight. He was the seventh child of nine born to William and Martha Knowlton. Located in northeastern Connecticut and bisected by the Mount Hope River, Ashford was a relatively new settlement, founded in 1714. The family farm, located not far from the village church, provided the perfect vista of scenic rolling hills that would eventually be known as the "Quiet Corner." Of his siblings, Thomas remained close to his second-oldest brother, Daniel (born 1738), who would also serve in the French and Indian War and that of the Revolution; they would serve together in Captain Jedediah Fay's Tenth Company, Third Connecticut Regiment, from May 1, 1758, to November 20, 1758.[78]

Following a rigorous campaign, the eighteen-year-old returned home to take the hand of Anna Keyes, daughter of Sampson Keyes of Ashford, on April 5, 1759.[79] Before the two could get settled, however, duty again called. Knowlton rose quickly through the ranks and was a lieutenant by March 1762. After his formidable exploits in Havana, he returned home to raise a family, replacing his musket with a plow until the Lexington alarm.[80]

Battle of Bunker Hill

By special order of the governor, the General Assembly of Connecticut met on April 26, 1775, and ordered one-fourth of the militia ready for active service. The one-hundred-man Ashford Company, under newly elected Captain Knowlton, was mobilized and ordered to Boston.[81]

On the night of June 16, Knowlton led a detachment composed of 120 men drafted from four companies of Putnam's regiment over Bunker Hill to Breed's Hill, an elevation closer to the city of Boston. To the east was Moulton's Point, at the end of the peninsula; the village of Charlestown lay south on the Charles River, and to the north, at about four hundred yards, flowed the Mystic.

There an effective breastwork was created out of fencing, allowing the detachment to hold its ground against the advancing British grenadiers. Miraculously, only three from Knowlton's company died in a battle that saw over two hundred British casualties. A later battle assessment asserted, "The utter disregard by both sides of plain dictates of prudence, for the obstinate valor of the combatants, and for its moral effect at home and abroad."[82]

This statue honors General Israel Putnam, regarded by Washington as one of America's most valuable military assets. Putnam also handled some secret dispatches from the Culper Ring.

A stoic Knowlton, soon to be addressed as major, had stood tall even when the gun he was using was shot from his hand; so powerful was the display that Washington avowed the name "Knowlton" and took his company for the unpretentious position as his bodyguard.

1776

The shadow of reconciliation fading, Major Knowlton led his men in a successful incursion into Charlestown on the evening of January 8, 1776. There he put fire to housing used by British officers and took a handful of prisoners in tow. Completed without injury or the discharging of a firearm, it was a firm statement. British general William Howe, in good sense, evacuated Boston on March 17.

The campaign then shifted to New York City, where Washington had directed the Continental forces to rendezvous. As surmised, the enemy arrived during the summer with an estimated force of over twenty thousand

Mixer Tavern, built in 1710, was a popular haunt for many an Ashford Patriot.

men supported by fleet. Aware of the dangers that awaited, Knowlton stopped at home during his southern march. While some of his men relaxed at Mixer Tavern, he retired into Anna's arms; it would be the last time he would see his wife and young children.

On August 12, Thomas Knowlton was appointed lieutenant colonel of the Twentieth Regiment. His successful excursions led to the formation of the Connecticut, or "Knowlton's," Rangers. Encompassing volunteers from five Connecticut, one Rhode Island and two Massachusetts regiments, it was an elite group and America's first intelligence unit; the roster also included Knowlton's son and brother. Among its captains were Stephen Brown of Ashford, Thomas Grosvenor of Pomfret and Nathan Hale of Coventry, all capable men of extraordinary courage.

New York was a complicated set of chess moves, and it began with the Battle of Brooklyn—later known as the Battle of Long Island—fought on August 27, 1776. In the first move to control the strategically important city, the British would prevail; the largest battle of the entire conflict, it was a downright debacle. The withdrawal from Brooklyn on the evening of August 29 left General George Washington feeling foolish, inept and short of tactical information. The commander in chief looked to Knowlton, who then turned to his nonpareil band of brothers.

Volunteering to go behind enemy lines and report on British troop movements would be Captain Nathan Hale; he accepted the mission on September 8 and was ferried into position four days later. British forces crossed from Long Island to occupy Montresor's Island, at the mouth of the Harlem River, on September 10. On Sunday, September 15, under a heavy cannonade, the British then landed above New York City on the East River (about 105th Street), near Kip's Bay. From the crest of Harlem Heights, Washington's new command post, he could hear the cannons and see the smoke. A successful British invasion was imminent.

Before daybreak the next morning, Knowlton's Rangers, outfitted as a regiment of light infantry, were given the task to scout the British advance. Cautiously making his way through the woods south at Harlem Heights, Knowlton halted his team and sent forward two scouts. The goal of inconspicuous movement was suddenly abandoned when the duo was forced to discharge their muskets. Spotted by the pickets of elite enemy infantry, a vicious fight ensued. The Rangers, vastly outnumbered, retreated and made a stand.

Adjutant General Joseph Reed, who had witnessed the fighting with the Rangers, then returned to Washington's headquarters to request reinforcements. The commander in chief ordered three companies of Colonel Weedon's regiment from Virginia, under the command of Major Andrew Leitch, to join force with the Rangers to try to get to the enemy's rear while a disposition was feinting a frontal assault. The goal was to trap the enemy in the Hollow Way, a topographical depression at about 129th Street and Broadway.

But the plan unraveled. Knowlton's forces attacked too soon, hitting the enemy's flank instead of getting behind and cutting off their retreat. As the fighting intensified, both Knowlton and Leitch fell mortally wounded.

Undeterred, the Rangers and sharpshooters advanced slowly during hours of fighting. Finally, the British took flight, and the attack was called off. Washington would later define it as a "a pretty sharp skirmish."[83]

Two men stepped forward to assist the mortally wounded Knowlton: Colonel Joseph Reed, who would remark, "When gasping in the agonies of death all his inquiry was if we had drove the enemy," and Captain Stephen Brown, who stated, "The ball entered the small of his back.[84] I took hold of him and asked if he were badly wounded. He told me he was, but, says he, 'I do not value my life if we do but get the day.' He seemed as unconcerned and calm as though nothing had happened." Colonel Knowlton was buried with full military honors in an unmarked grave west of Ninth Avenue, near 143rd Street.

POSTSCRIPT

The Knowlton family burial plot in Warrenville in the town of Ashford.

A Knowlton monument stands in Snow Cemetery in Ashford.[85] Anna Knowlton died on May 22, 1808, at the age of sixty-four. Colonel Thomas Knowlton is also acknowledged at the family burial plot in Westford Hill Cemetery.

Washington, who for nearly fifteen months had relied so heavily on his judgment and valor, was despondent. In his general orders for September 17, 1776, he stated, "The gallant and brave Col Knowlton…would have been an Honor to any Country, having fallen yesterday, while gloriously fighting." Years later, Colonel Aaron Burr said, "I had a full account of the Battle [Bunker Hill] from Knowlton's own lips, and I believe if the chief command had been entrusted to him, the issue would have proved more fortunate. It was impossible to promote such a man too rapidly."[86]

Knowlton is depicted, wearing a white shirt and holding a musket, in John Trumbull's powerful painting *The Death of General Warren at the Battle of Bunker Hill, June 17, 1775.* The work was also a source for Enoch S. Wood's brilliant statue that rests outside the statehouse in Hartford, Connecticut.

The memory of Thomas Knowlton remains at the forefront of American intelligence gathering. The LTC Thomas W. Knowlton Award was established in 1995 by the Military Intelligence Corps Association. It recognizes those individuals who have contributed significantly to the promotion of army military intelligence. Also, the date "1776" on the modern U.S. Army's intelligence service seal refers to the formation of Knowlton's Rangers.

Chapter 7
Benedict Arnold

A traitor is everyone who does not agree with me.
—George III

In September 1780, General George Washington alerted Major General Benedict Arnold that he would pass "secretly" through the Hudson Valley bound for Hartford.[87] The pensive and unassuming commander in chief—who had announced on August 3, 1780, that Arnold would take control of the garrison at West Point, located on the west bank of the Hudson River—was hoping to reinvigorate his spirits with a visit to the improved fortress. Naturally, the presence alone of perhaps his most gifted subordinate, Washington thought, would certainly bolster his emotional state; the principal who stood proudly with Ethan Allen at Fort Ticonderoga and fought heroically at Saratoga was, above all, a paragon of fearless leadership.

The image of Benedict Arnold as depicted by artist John Trumbull. *LC-USZ62-68483.*

But instead of preparing for the classified arrival, Arnold relayed the information to the enemy—an action that, had it been timely, might have put Washington in peril. Despondency over his personal affairs had prompted Arnold to barter through a discreet correspondence with General Clinton's staff: his patriotism for a bounty and alternative command. It was a dynamic transformation that had reached the point of no return.

A Connecticut Turncoat

Since February 1777, Arnold had been bitter.[88] That's when the Congress passed him over in naming five new major generals, all brigadiers junior to him and, in his mind, no more qualified. Even though Washington had eased his pain by assisting him in becoming a major general, it was too little, too late. Nor was it enough to be named military commandant of Philadelphia following the British evacuation of June 1778, even if it did include a rather opulent lifestyle, complete with a trophy wife.

The effervescent Margaret "Peggy" Shippen, Arnold's second consort and half his age, was born into a prominent Philadelphia family and quickly gained a reputation for being, let's say, free-spirited.[89] While the British occupied the city, she occupied the British. Married within months of their introduction, the Arnolds created an atmosphere—overtly Loyalist-friendly—that appeared a bit too self-serving for most. Allegations quickly arose—fueled by the executive council of Pennsylvania, presided over by Joseph Reed, Arnold's persistent nemesis—and when they reached routine tavern gossip, action needed to be taken. Arnold demanded a court-martial to clear his name, and that request was granted.[90] Found guilty—"peculiarly reprehensible, both in a civil and military view"—of two of four charges of malfeasance, he faced his punishment: a mild reprimand. It was, however, a Washington admonishment, as a result of the incident, that most historians feel turned Arnold.

Benedict Arnold V, born on January 14, 1741, in Norwich, appeared compact—short, more torso than legs and with a dark complexion. He was the second of six children born to the Connecticut family of Benedict Arnold III and Hannah Waterman King.[91] Named after his great-grandfather, an early colonial governor of Rhode Island, Arnold was intelligent, enterprising and a bit mischievous; his father, who suffered from problems with alcohol, found his son difficult to control. As a teenager, he witnessed the passing of

The grave of Benedict's mother, Hannah King Arnold, in the family burial plot in Norwichtown, Connecticut. At eighteen, Benedict Arnold stood in this very spot.

his siblings, a family bankruptcy and the death of his mother. Although he apprenticed in Lathrop's apothecary shop and worked as a pharmacist and bookseller in New Haven, he never forgot his childhood struggles. Drawn to the water—and the treasures it could bear—he later became a successful merchant. No wave was too high and no depth too low for this pugnacious sea captain.

In May 1779, Arnold sent for Philadelphia Loyalist Joseph Stansbury. It would be Stansbury, assisted by cryptologist Reverend Jonathan Odell, who would travel to New York to inform the enemy of Arnold's British overtures. When the information reached Major John André, the British spy and aide-de-camp of General Henry Clinton, the foundation for betrayal was set. The pair, Arnold and André, then began communicating through secret code to avoid detection—the cipher key being one of two choices, either Blackstone's *Commentaries on the Laws of England* or *Nathan Bailey's Dictionary*, both standard published works.[92] No word would be directly written in letter, only a code in the form of a page, line and word number. Posing as merchants in their correspondence to avoid detection, they would later schedule a discreet rendezvous.

On September 21, 1780, André found himself behind enemy lines, accepting from Arnold what would prove to be his death warrant: papers outlining West Point's troop and artillery strength, along with the sensitive September 6 War Council minutes.[93] When circumstance would not allow André to return to the British sloop *Vulture*, he was forced to escape overland. Into André's boots the documents went, along with a letter of pass for Mr.

The treason of Arnold as portrayed in a later engraving. *LC-DIG-ppmsca-30575.*

John Anderson (his code name), penned by the prescient Arnold. Safety, obviously, was of paramount concern to both.

Two days later, three Westchester County militiamen stopped and stripped an individual of concern. André had aroused suspicion with his immaculate dress, a sleek purple coat lined with gold trim. When the prestigious set of documents was uncovered, action needed to be taken. They were turned over to the nearest officer, acting commander Lieutenant Colonel John Jameson, who then conveyed them to Washington, while André was sent under guard to Arnold's headquarters. Learning of the incident and recognizing the name, Benjamin Tallmadge—a military intelligence czar who had personally been leading area patrols in preparation for Washington's meeting with the distinguished French officer Rochambeau—persuaded Jameson to have André brought back. However, the incident report on the way to Arnold could not be stopped.

Washington, still unaware of the event, was en route to the Arnold home.[94] Sending word ahead of his impeding arrival, the group reached the Arnold home, two miles from West Point, on the morning of September 25. There they were informed by Arnold aides that the commander had been summoned to the fort and that Mrs. Arnold lay in repose in her upstairs chamber. Following a quick breakfast, Washington moved to inspect West Point, which he found in appalling condition. Returning in late afternoon, it was just before dinner that the damning papers arrived at the very home of the defector. So startled by the news, Washington's voice was barely audible: "Arnold has betrayed us!"[95]

As felicitous as it was implausible, Arnold learned of André's capture just prior to his superior's arrival.

The actual first page of the letter sent by Arnold while he was on board the sloop *Vulture* on September 25, 1780. *GWP-LC.*

Abruptly departing his residence, he withdrew north on the Hudson River to evade his own capture, and hopefully find solace—as André had expected to do—aboard the *Vulture*. Meanwhile, Peggy Arnold, clad only in a loose dressing gown, was playing the role of victim to perfection. Washington let her be, secured the premise and then moved to fortify West Point in case of attack.

As if to fuel the flames of disloyalty, Washington then received a pair of letters from the scoundrel himself. In the first, an abrasive Arnold tried to acquit himself of his actions—complete with a concierge's request to arrange for his baggage—while declaring his wife's innocence of any wrongdoing. The second letter, addressed to his wife, was delivered to her quarters. Forever the gentlemen, Washington acknowledged Arnold's petition and even guaranteed Peggy's safe passage to her father's home in Philadelphia.

THE EXALTED JOHN ANDRÉ

The aristocratic swagger of John André was alluring yet dangerous. Born on May 2, 1750, in London, he was the son of successful merchant Antoine André of Geneva, Switzerland, and his wife, Marie Louise Giradot, from Paris. Charming, well educated and handsome, he turned to the military at the age of twenty. As a member of the British army, he spent time in Canada; it was there, in 1775, that he was captured and then removed to a Lancaster, Pennsylvania prison. Following the granting of his freedom as part of a prisoner exchange, he was aggressively promoted.

During the British occupation of Philadelphia, André quickly fell into favor as part of the colonial society—a renaissance man in the truest sense of the word. His efficiency had landed him an appointment as deputy adjutant general on the staff of General Henry Clinton, the British commander in chief, as well as his trust and a future role in espionage. Handling all British intelligence by April 1779, André had begun plotting with General Arnold, some believe through an intimate relationship with Peggy Shippen Arnold.

Upon his capture, André had little recourse other than to play the British officer's card; spies, as common criminals, were hanged, while a uniformed officer in contact with a spy faced a firing squad. Naturally, the latter was a more befitting, so he thought, sentence for his actions. Washington, not captivated by his prisoner's allure or appeal, placed his prisoner on trial in a village church in Tappan, New York. A distinguished military panel would determine his fate.

On September 29, 1780, the Board of General Officers—a majority of the fourteen with Connecticut connections—convened. Despite the significant impression André had made with his frank and eloquent remarks, the board returned a verdict of guilty. The spy would hang, despite pleas for a firing squad.

Washington was overrun by calls for mercy. Arnold himself—for whom Washington tried to barter a prisoner trade—pleaded, as did his own staff.[96] Yet the verdict stood. In full view of soldiers drawn from various quarters of the army, John André, reconciled to his fate, marched to the gallows at noon on October 2, 1780. His final words: "Nothing but to request you will witness to the world that I die like a brave man."

To this very day, John André is revered as the prototypical spy. At the behest of the Duke of York, his remains, which had been buried under the gallows, were removed to London in 1821 and placed among those of nobility in Hero's Corner at Westminster Abbey. A monument, with a detailed inscription, rests at the site of the hanging.

André's captors—John Paulding, Isaac Van Wart and David Williams— were given a pension of $200 a year and a silver medal, known as the Fidelity Medallion; a monument still stands where they captured the spy.

CODICIL

Given a British brigadier general's commission after the treason, Arnold would begin a rampage of Virginia in December 1780 and then turn his sights toward Connecticut. On September 4, 1781, he raided and burned New London and captured Fort Griswold. But the casualties exceeded expectations, and Arnold was essentially dismissed by his peers. The Arnolds departed New York for England on December 8, 1781, though even there he could not escape his tarnished reputation.

As the century concluded, Arnold's health began failing, his war-weary legs barely able to support his body. He passed away on June 14, 1801, at the age of sixty; he would be buried at St. Mary's Church, Battersea, in London, alongside Peggy Shippen Arnold—who died three years later, having borne her husband five children who survived until adulthood—and daughter Sophia Matilda Phipps.

As for Arnold's legacy, "traitor" seems to define it to most. In Connecticut, however, many still recall the old Franklin line: "Judas sold only one man, Arnold three million."[97]

Chapter 8

Edward Bancroft

Dr. [Edward] Bancroft…you will find [to be] a very intelligent, sensible man, well acquainted with the state of affairs here, and who has heretofore been employed in the service of Congress. I have long known him, and esteem him highly.
—*Benjamin Franklin, in a 1783 letter to Robert Livingston*

If anyone understood the percipient Bancroft, it certainly must have been Franklin, the man who appointed, worked with and defended him in his role as secretary to the American commissioners in Paris.[98] Often appearing brilliant to a fault, Franklin just might have been. Sixty-eight years after the death of Edward Bancroft, he was unmasked as a spy, having masterfully conducted himself right underneath the muzzle of the good doctor.

One of two sons, Bancroft was born on January 9, 1744, to a Massachusetts farming family.[99] His parents were Edward Bancroft, of Westfield, and Mary Ely, of Springfield, Massachusetts, and together they settled in Westfield, the westernmost settlement in the Massachusetts colony. While still an infant, Edward's father died tragically of an epileptic seizure on the family farm; he was just twenty-eight years old. Mary, along with her two sons, tended to what she could, but life wasn't easy. In January 1751, she married David Bull. The family moved several times before finally settling in Hartford, Connecticut, where Edward's stepfather opened the Bunch of Grapes tavern. In a bit of historical irony, a young Silas Deane was hired to tutor Edward; although the length of Bancroft's instruction was short, the introduction would prove inestimable.

In the autumn of 1760, the Bancroft family moved to Killingworth, Connecticut, where Edward would apprentice with a local physician. Later,

A lithograph of Franklin's reception at the court of France, 1778. *LC-USZC4-623.*

he would skip out of the apprenticeship and set sail for some exotic southern destinations; in locations such as Barbados and Guiana, he would combine his love for medicine with that of botany and chemistry. Finally returning to Hartford in the summer of 1766, his stay would be brief—no doubt just long enough to satisfy the conditions of his abandoned apprenticeship. The following February, Bancroft traveled to Great Britain.

London proved a wealth of opportunities for the aspirant Bancroft. He studied medicine and published a natural history book in 1769, which caught the attention of Paul Wentworth, New Hampshire's colonial agent in London, who offered him employment on his Surinam plantation. As ironic as the Deane association would prove, add to it that of Wentworth, Arthur Lee's irregular friend. Bancroft also met Benjamin Franklin. Striking up a strong friendship based primarily on their shared scientific interests, the young man agreed to gather intelligence for the elder colonist.[100]

A FRENCH CONNECTION

When the Committee of Secret Correspondence sent agent Silas Deane to France in 1776, it was Franklin—who had left London two years earlier—who suggested he contact Bancroft. More than happy to accept the role of unofficial secretary to his former tutor, the gregarious Bancroft—who spoke French fluently while Deane did not—was immediately effective to the agent's negotiations.

However, when Deane expressed thoughts of Britain engaging in a war with not only America but also others, including France, Bancroft grew concerned. He was a British American, in favor of reconciliation, not conflict. In the summer of 1776, he decided to return to London and meet with members of the British Secret Service, including a recruit, Paul Wentworth. With a wealth of consternation, Bancroft resigned himself to the role of double agent.

Franklin's arrival back to France to assist Deane affirmed Bancroft's secretarial appointment to the American Commission in Paris; he would serve in this capacity—to the delight of the British Secret Service—until peace was at hand. Fulfilling his duties to perfection, Bancroft was also able to establish good pretext for frequent excursions to England, where he maintained a residence, and efficient cover. At one point, he even arranged for his false arrest. Of the three colonial commissioners, only Arthur Lee questioned the loyalty of Franklin's protégé. Unfortunately, it was ignored.

In his stealth role, Bancroft—who didn't always like what he heard, and he perceived everything—typically remained taciturn; only the consumption of Burgundy could loosen his tongue. With a vast range of expertise in chemistry, including unusual avocations in the areas of invisible inks and even poisons, Bancroft penned weekly reports under the moniker of "Edward Edwards." Every Tuesday, he put the chemically disguised messages inside bottles and left them in a hole in a certain box tree in Paris, located at the present-day south terrace of the Tuileries, a formal garden next to the Louvre. After 9:30 p.m., a British official would retrieve the note and replace it with a new set of orders. (Lord Stormont, British ambassador to France and the recipient of the information, possessed the ink developer required to read the note.) Bancroft would then return to recover the bottle. It has been said that this is the method by which George III saw the French-American Treaty of Alliance just days after it had been signed. *Voila!*[101]

Playwright turned secret agent Pierre Beaumarchais was the first to discern the accurate flow of information in and out of the Hotel de

A La Memoire de Charles Gravier Comte de Vergennes in Versaille, France. Gravier is, without question, the most overlooked figure of the American Revolution.

Valentinois, where the commissioners lived and Bancroft worked. Versailles, too, noticed, in particular the able-bodied French minister Charles Gravier, comte de Vergennes, who fingered not Bancroft but Arthur Lee—Deane's nemesis—as the intelligence source.

AFTERTHOUGHT

Regardless of his expertise, Bancroft did not prevent the French-American Alliance.[102]

As might be surmised, there has been endless debate as to whether Franklin knew Bancroft was a spy. The gifted polymath wrote that he suspected one associate of being a British spy but remained confident that the situation was under control.[103] If Franklin ever suspected Bancroft, he remained silent; when you think about it, what other choice did he have?

After the Revolution, Bancroft became wealthy through patents he had obtained. He also published another book and was elected a foreign honorary member of the American Academy of Arts and Sciences in 1797 before passing on September 8, 1821, in Margate, Kent, England. When his diplomatic papers were released to the public in 1889, his role as a double agent was unearthed. Along with being recognized as an accomplished spy, he was living proof of Franklin's own philosophy: "To follow by faith alone is to follow blindly."

Chapter 9
David Bushnell and Ezra Lee

The skillful operator can swim so low on the surface of the water, as to approach very near a ship in the night, without fear of being discovered; and may, if he choose, approach the stern or stem, above water, with very little danger. He can sink very quickly, keep at any necessary depth, and row a great distance in any direction he desires without coming to the surface. When he rises to the surface, he can soon obtain a fresh supply of air, and, if necessary, he may then descend again and pursue his course.[104]
—David Bushnell, 1799

The *Turtle* was the creation of Connecticut native David Bushnell, who saw the craft as "two upper tortoise shells of equal size, joined together." Born on August 30, 1740, in Saybrook, to Nehemiah and Sarah Ingham Bushnell, he was the eldest of four siblings. As a mature undergraduate at Yale (1771–75), his design included the basic requirements for a successful submersible: the ability to go under water, the aptness to maneuver submerged, the potential to maintain an adequate air supply to support the operator of the craft, the power to carry out effective offensive operations against an enemy surface vessel and a functional operator interface.[105] Upon completion, the final and perhaps most critical component would be the selection of a qualified pilot.

With custom-designed assemblies and innovative subassemblies, its simple exterior masked a far more complex interior. The *Turtle* broke new ground with the inclusion of a breathing mechanism, the use of water as ballast for raising and lowering the submersible, the addition of a screw propeller and

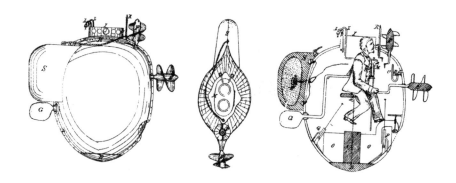

This print shows three views of the *Turtle*, a one-man submarine designed and built by David Bushnell. *LC-USZ62-110384.*

the incorporation of a "torpedo" or mine. As the first to demonstrate that gunpowder could be exploded under water, Bushnell now had an efficient delivery system.

According to Bushnell:

> *The external appearance of the torpedo bears some resemblance to two upper tortoise shells, of equal size, placed in contact, leaving at that part which represents the head of the animal, a flue or opening, sufficiently capacious to contain the operator, and air to support him thirty minutes. At the bottom, opposite to the entrance, is placed a quantity of lead for ballast. The operator sits upright, and holds an oar for rowing forward or backward, and is furnished with a rudder for steering. An aperture at the bottom, with its valve, admits water for the purpose of descending, and two brass forcing pumps serve to eject the water within, when necessary for ascending.*[106]

It's not difficult to imagine Bushnell, a detail-driven individual, providing meticulous attention to each component of his extraordinary watercraft.

> *The vessel is made completely water-tight, furnished with glass windows for the admission of light, with ventilators and air-pipes, and is so ballasted, with lead fixed at the bottom, as to render it solid, and obviate all danger of oversetting. Behind the submarine vessel, is a place above the rudder*

for carrying a large powder magazine; this is made of two pieces of oak timber, large enough, when hollowed out, to contain one hundred and fifty pounds of powder, with the apparatus used for firing it, and is secured in its place by a screw turned by the operator. It is lighter than water, that it may rise against the object to which it is intended to be fastened. Within the magazine, is an apparatus constructed to run any proposed length of time under twelve hours; when it has run out its time, it unpinions a strong lock, resembling a gun-lock, which gives fire to the powder. This apparatus is so pinioned, that it cannot possibly move, till, by casting off the magazine from the vessel, it is set in motion.

When the Lexington alarm reached Bushnell, he became incensed; he could not suppress the thought of his device as a warship targeted at the British Royal Navy. Though project secrecy was paramount, it was also improbable. Cost and significance were two reasons, and the thought of hostilities was now a third.

In pursuit of an appropriation, Dr. Benjamin Gale (1715–1790) of Killingworth, Connecticut, a Bushnell friend and Yale instructor, would write on November 9, 1775, to Silas Deane, a member of the Congress from Connecticut who served on the Continental Marine Committee:

Lately he [Bushnell] *has conducted matters and his designs with the greatest secrecy, both for the personal safety of the navigator as to produce the greatest astonishment to those against whom it is designed. If this projection succeeds, of which I make no doubt, as I well know the man and have seen the machine while in embryo, and every addition made to it fills me with fresh astonishment and surprize. And you may call me a visionary, an enthusiast, or what you please, I do insist upon it, that I believe the inspiration of the Almighty has given him understanding for this very purpose and design. If he succeeds, a stipend for life, and if he fails, a reasonable compensation for time and expense is his due from the public.*[107]

In a subsequent letter to Deane, thirteen days later, Dr. Gale confirms Franklin's visit to Connecticut and his interest in the project, writing, "I had not seen him [Bushnell] myself since Dr. Franklin was here." Franklin, whose actions were never short of attracting attention, certainly would have aroused some interest in Killingworth. Every wall, at this time, had ears.

A coded message to William Tryon, the last royal governor of the Province of New York, brought Bushnell's work to the attention of the British; the element of surprise was no longer.[108] While some may recall Tryon as one of a group of conspirators who would bungle a plot to kidnap George Washington and to assassinate his chief officers in the summer of 1776, Connecticut residents typically remember the scoundrel at the Battle of Ridgefield, where he defeated General David Wooster and Benedict Arnold. If Tryon had any information that would assist the Crown, you could be certain it got into the proper hands.

Weeks later, on Friday, February 2, 1776, Bushnell attended a meeting of the governor and Council of Safety in Lebanon, Connecticut. He was not only acknowledged but also supported by both. Governor Jonathan Trumbull affirmed the group's position:

> *Mr. [David] Bushnell was here, by request of the Governor and Council, and gave an account of his machine contrived to blow ships &c., and was asked many questions about it &c. &c., and being retired, on consideration, voted, that we hold ourselves under obligations of secrecy about it. And, his Honor the D. Governor is desired to reward him for his trouble and expence in coming here, and signifie to him that we approve of his plan and that [it] will be agreeable to have him proceed to make every necessary preparation and experiment about it, with expectation of proper public notice and reward.*[109]

Overseer Jonathan Trumbull Sr.—never more than paper, post rider and a few (quill) dips from the commander in chief of the Continental army—would ensure that the inventor's work would not be overlooked. Additional financing, he believed, would ensure its progress. Navigation efficiency, as documented in Bushnell's notes, had yet to be perfected.

Of the inventor, Washington would retrospectively pen, "A man of great Mechanical powers—fertile of invention—and a master in execution. He came to me in 1776 recommended by Governor Trumbull and other respectable characters who were proselites to his plan."[110]

EZRA LEE

Born in August 1749 in Lyme, Connecticut, Ezra Lee was son to Abner and Elizabeth Lee. Just before his twenty-sixth birthday, he joined the Connecticut Line of the Continental army. Sent to New York in August

1776, he patrolled Long Island Sound from Throg Neck to York Island. The following month, he was selected by General Samuel Holden Parsons, also of Lyme and a former member of Connecticut's Council of Safety, to learn how to operate the *Turtle*; Bushnell's brother Ezra, initially slated for the first duty of the device, had fallen ill.

THE FIRST MISSION: SEPTEMBER 6, 1776

It was General George Washington himself who authorized an attack on British admiral Richard Howe's flagship HMS *Eagle*, then lying in New York Harbor. With Lee at the controls of the *Turtle*, here was Bushnell's reflection:

He went under the Ship and attempted to fix the Woodscrew into her bottom, but struck as he supposes, a bar of iron, which passes from the rudder hinge and is spiked under the Ship's quarter. Had he moved a few

A replica of the first operational submarine, the *Turtle*, built in Westbrook, Connecticut, in 1775. This reproduction can be found inside the Connecticut River Museum.

inches, which he might have done without rowing, I have no doubt, but he would have found wood, where he might have fixed the screw; or if the Ship were sheathed with copper, he might easily have pierced it: but, not being well skilled in the management of the Vessel, in attempting to move to another place, he lost the Ship. After seeking her in vain, for some time, he rowed some distance, and rose to the surface of the water, but found daylight had advanced so far, that he durst not renew the attempt.[111]

He says that he could easily have fastened the Magazine under the Stern of the Ship, above water, as he rowed up to the stern, and touched it, before he descended. Had he fastened it there, the explosion of one hundred and fifty pounds of powder, the quantity contained in the Magazine, must have been fatal to the Ship. In his return from the Ship to N. York, he passed near Governor's Island, and thought he was discovered by the Enemy, on the Island; being in hast to avoid the danger he feared, he cast off the magazine, as he imagined it retarded him, in the swell, which was very considerable. After the Magazine had been cast off, one hour, the time the internal apparatus was set to run, it blew up with great violence.[112]

Bushnell would also recall:

Afterwards there were two attempts made in Hudson's River above the City, but they effected nothing. One of them was by the aforementioned person. In going toward the Ship, he lost sight of her, and went a great distance beyond her, before he found her; when he arrived, the tide ran so strong, that as he descended under water, for the Ship's bottom, it swept him away.[113]

Soon after this, the Enemy went up the river, and pursued the boat, which had the submarine Vessel on board, and sunk it, with their shot. After I recovered the Vessel, I found it impossible, at that time to prosecute the design any farther.[114]

A dejected Bushnell continues:

I had been in a bad state of health from the beginning of my undertaking, and was now very unwell; the situation of public affairs was such, that I despaired of obtaining the public attention, and the assistance necessary. I was unable to support myself, and the persons I must have employed, had I proceeded. Beside I found it absolutely necessary, that the operators should, acquire more skill in the management of the Vessel, before I could expect success; which would have taken up sometime, and made no small additional expence. I therefore gave over the pursuit, for that time, and waited for a more favourable opportunity, which never arrived.[115]

The heartfelt admission, while ex post facto, is a clear indication of his frustration with the device and its operator.

LEE'S ASSESSMENT FROM DOWN UNDER

Intriguing is the comparison of perspectives between inventor and user, or operator, if you will: "Unmanageable in a swell or a strong tide." This the only criticism vented by Ezra Lee in a February 20, 1815 note to Connecticut-born David Humphreys. For such a rare and dangerous undertaking, Lee was not to fault Bushnell—even decades later—for the mission's failure.

Inside a replica of Bushnell's *Turtle*, showing the many controls necessary to successfully operate the submersible. This reproduction can be found inside the Connecticut River Museum.

In explanatory notations, apparently added by Humphreys and likely bound for a book, the apparent cause of the failure is clarified: "The reason why the screw would not enter, was that the ship's bottom being coppered it would have been difficult under any circumstances to have pierced through it...but on attempting to bore with the auger, the force necessary to be used in pressing against the ships bottom, caused the machine to rebound off this difficulty defeated the whole...the screw could not enter the bottom, and of course the magazine could not be kept there in the mode desired."[116]

Additional Bushnell Attempts

Bushnell reminisced:

In the year 1777, I made an attempt; from a Whaleboat, against the Cerberus Frigate, then lying at anchor, between Connecticut River & New London, by drawing a Machine against her side, by means of a line. The Machine was loaded with Powder, to be exploded by a gunlock, which was to be unpinioned by an apparatus, to be turned by being brought along the side of the Frigate. This Machine fell in with a schooner, at anchor astern of the Frigate, & concealed from my sight. By some means or other it was fired, and demolished the schooner, and three men, and blew the only one left alive, overboard, who was taken up very much hurt.[117]

After this, I fixed several Keggs under water, charged with powder, to explode upon touching anything, as they floated along with the tide: I set them afloat in the Delaware, above the English shipping at Philadelphia, in December 1777. I was unacquainted with the River, and obliged to depend upon a Gentleman, very imperfectly acquainted with that part of it, as I afterwards found. We went as near the shipping as he durst venture; I believe the darkness of the night greatly deceived him, as it did me. We set them adrift, to fall with the ebb upon the Shipping. Had we been within sixty rods, I believe they must have fallen in with them immediately as I designed; but, as I afterwards found, they were set adrift much too far distant, and did not arrive, until after being detained some time by frost, they advanced in the day time in a dispersed situation, and under great disadvantage. One of them blew up a boat, with several persons in it, who imprudently handled it too freely, and thus gave the British that alarm, which brought on the battle of the Keggs.[118]

Coda

No worse for his maritime exploits, Ezra Lee would go on to distinguish himself often on the battlefield. After his service, the respected veteran returned to Lyme, where he died on October 9, 1821. Ezra Lee is buried in the Duck River Cemetery, also known as the Old Lyme Cemetery, in Old Lyme, Connecticut.

Bushnell was appointed a captain-lieutenant in the Corps of Sappers and Miners—a predecessor to the modern-day Corps of Engineers—in the Continental army in August 1779. He also saw battle at Yorktown, Virginia. Mustered out of the army in 1783, Bushnell, who suffered from bouts of depression and illness, returned to Saybrook. Four years later, he abruptly disappeared. Following his death in January or early February 1826, it was learned that he had settled in Columbia County, Georgia. There, as David Bush, he purchased land, became a commissioner and even practiced as a physician in 1818. He is believed to be interred in an unmarked grave in the Warrenton Cemetery in Warrenton, Georgia.

The grave of *Turtle* pilot Ezra Lee, who tried to destroy a portion of the Royal Navy in New York Harbor.

Groton, Connecticut, on the Thames River, is home to the Naval Submarine Base New London and General Dynamics Electric Boat, the major contractor for submarine work for the United States Navy. Having become synonymous with the word "submarine," Groton is also home to the U.S. Navy Submarine Force Library and Museum.[119]

Chapter 10

Enoch Crosby

I know but little of the customs of war, and wish to know less.
—*James Fenimore Cooper,* The Spy

Appearing in a new literary genre, Harvey Birch, a fictional spy, so captured the imagination of readers that some even claimed to have seen the figure traveling through the hills and valleys of Westchester County. The character was that vivid! And, if not for Birch, the name Enoch Crosby, a real spy, might have slipped into obscurity.

THE BIRCH MYSTIQUE

Enoch Crosby's exploits during the American Revolution were so similar to the hero of James Fenimore Cooper's 1821 novel *The Spy: A Tale of the Neutral Ground* that most considered him the same person. Indeed, the proximity, characters and events are difficult to contest—a comparison well beyond this introduction—but transforming the role of an intelligence officer into a "cool, shrewd and fearless by nature figure," which Harvey Birch was, according to Cooper, took the imagination and pen of a gifted fiction writer. And that is precisely what we have here…or do we?

A supposed Loyalist, Birch, the protagonist in the author's second novel, spied for George Washington. It's a fascinating adventure filled with swelling rhetoric and devout nationalism—a perfect period piece. Shifting comfortably between the Continental and British armies,

Harvey Birch, seen holding a cloth draped over his arms, so captured the imagination of readers that some actually claimed to have seen the figure. *LC-USZ62-112531.*

the plot finds quarters in the historic setting of Westchester County, New York.

Cooper's source for the character came from his conversations with an old friend, the distinguished diplomat John Jay. Having had occasion to employ a spy or two as a member of the Committee for Detecting and Defeating Conspiracies, Jay was certainly familiar with the role and more than willing to share a few accounts with his Cooperstown companion. All ears, Cooper became fascinated with the profession, its complexity and the challenge of making such a character believable; remember, we're trying to sell books here. Harvey Birch, a mirror image of Jay's ideal intelligence officer, was quick to find a home in the author's narrative.

Success breeds association, and when *The Spy* became a bestseller, many individuals came forward to claim they were the prototype for the fictional character. But none was like that of regional operative Enoch Crosby, whose proclamation was firm: *he* was Harvey Birch! From taking a bow at the revived 1826 stage presentation of the work to an intriguing, if not romanticized, biography by H.L. Barnum titled *The Spy Unmasked; or, Memoirs of Enoch*

Crosby, alias Harvey Birch, Crosby fit the bill. More affirmation followed. His sworn 1832 deposition, in an attempt to secure a pension, was so powerful an affidavit that most historians rested their cases.

While Cooper's lasting reputation rests largely on his five Leatherstocking tales—*The Deerslayer*, *The Last of the Mohicans*, *The Pathfinder*, *The Pioneers* and *The Prairie*—perhaps we should also salute his persistence. Until his death in 1851, America's first successful novelist insisted that he never knew the name of Jay's agents, nor could he detail the life of Enoch Crosby. Spies, although clearly known to exist, were considered scandalous and far too dangerous a topic for literary discussion. Taking him at his word, Cooper must be hailed for his major literary gamble.[120]

Over time, Crosby's *accepted* account drew its fair share of detractors. Carving their initials into the legacy tree are James S. Diemer, who pointed to Henry Lee's *Memoirs of the War in the Southern Department of the United States* and the exploits of Sergeant John Champe; scholar Tremaine McDowell, who supported Cooper's claim of an original creation; noted New York State historian Frank Pennypacker, who attacked the evidence; and Professor Warren S. Walker, who rode Pennypacker's discovery, proclaiming "Samuel Culper" to be the prototype. The endless debate continues hollow haystack by hollow haystack, no doubt providing the ghost of James Fenimore Cooper more satisfaction than a summer sunrise over Otsego Lake.

Consistent with every argument, however, has been the evocation of a bona fide American hero, the name Enoch Crosby.

AN AMERICAN HERO

From a state of comfort and comparative affluence, the Crosby family suddenly found themselves reduced to poverty and distress. Crosby, at the age of seventy-eight, recalled the event for H.L. Barnum, his biographer: "I was compelled to leave the home of my childhood, to seek the protection of strangers, and depend upon my own exertions for support.[121] With the scanty outfit of a change of clothes, and a few shillings in my pocket, I bade a long adieu to the friends I best loved, and the scenes of my happiest days."

At the age of sixteen, Crosby's dedication led to a lengthy apprenticeship in Kent, New York, as a cordwainer (shoemaker)—it would be a useful skill as both an occupation and cover for his espionage exploits. Upon the completion of his term, he headed east to Danbury, Connecticut.

Enoch Crosby was born to Thomas and Elizabeth Crosby on June 5, 1750, in Harwich, Massachusetts. The family then moved to a picturesque farm in Southeast, Dutchess County (now Putnam County), New York, in 1753. Scarcely a day would pass—a time quoted by biographer Barnum but somewhat unbelievable considering the period—when the residents of the town were not fed some new accounts of distress being felt by their fellow colonists as a result of British suppression.[122]

Following the hostilities at Lexington and Concord in 1775, Enoch Crosby decided to enlist in the army. It was his time, he thought, to defend his rights and those of his countrymen.

IN SUPPORT OF SERVICE

On October 15, 1832, an eighty-two-year-old Enoch Crosby appeared before a Putnam County Clerk, in the state of New York, and signed a deposition to his service record.[123] This was part of an application for a federal pension. Duly sworn according to law, Crosby dictated a twelve-page public account. Recalling his employment as both soldier and spy—a valuable reference for anyone trying to draw comparisons between Crosby and Birch—he described his military service. Though the passage of time can omit or confuse many details, which is unfortunate, it also can filter or leave behind what the human mind finds least significant. It is fascinating how this hero, then an octogenarian, painted his self-portrait.

Crosby begins with a brief narrative of his first stint. It accounts for missions in New York and Canada—omitting details such as the length of battles, severe weather and sickness—before he was mustered out by December 13, 1775. His recollection improves, page by page, as the time passes.

On August 27, 1776, the unfortunate Battle of Long Island—the first major battle following the Declaration of Independence and the largest battle of the entire conflict—prompted a then twenty-seven-year-old Crosby to rejoin the fight. Described as "nearly six foot with broad shoulders, full chest and a liberal share of bone and muscle, but not a superabundance of flesh," he was an impressive, if not imposing, figure.[124] Crosby enlisted into the regiment commanded by Colonel Jacobus Swartout in Fredericksburgh, now Carmel in the County of Putnam. Having been unable to catch his new company before its departure, he left on foot, finding his way to a place in Westchester County in September.

Soon, Crosby fell into the company of an outsider by the name of Bunker, who mistook him for a Loyalist. While staying at the home of the stranger, Crosby gathered intelligence—names and meeting locations—on the raising of a local company whose plan was to soon join the British army. Sensing the urgency of the information, he discreetly parted company with the stranger to continue his journey.

As fate might have it, his next stop was an evening in the home of Patriot Joseph Young, whom Crosby learned was one of Westchester's commissioners of public safety. Feeling comfortable, Crosby communicated the vital information he had learned to Young. The gentlemen then asked Crosby to accompany him to White Plains the following morning to communicate this information to authorities. Crosby complied and, while there, explained that he was a solider trying to reach Colonel Jacobus Swartout's regiment. Sensing the level of urgency, the committee immediately sent a communication to the colonel requesting that Crosby remain there to assist in the apprehension of the organization, this being thought "more useful to his country."

For reasons of secrecy, Crosby posed as a prisoner and was ordered under the care of Captain Micah Townsend of Westchester, commander of Townsend's Rangers and a Loyalist hunter. As evening fell, the new prisoner made an excuse to step outside and then escaped. Traveling throughout the night, he finally reach Bunker's home, where he relayed the story, along with his request for protection. The following morning, Bunker introduced him to potential members of the new Loyalist group. As the days passed, Crosby gradually assimilated into his new environment. Just when the company was about complete, Crosby informed Young of the progress and its whereabouts. The group, about thirty in number including Crosby, was then taken prisoner and marched to White Plains. After a few days, the prisoners were finally ordered to Fishkill, in the county of Dutchess.

Now considered a suburb of New York City, the village of Fishkill was a recognized crossroads during the eighteenth century where the Kings Highway, connecting Albany to New York City, intersected with the major route from New England to the Hudson River. It was there that the Committee for Detecting Conspiracies was sitting. It was composed of statesman John Jay, politician and lawyer Zepaniah Platt, William Duer of the county of Albany and spymaster Nathaniel Sackett. The group had been briefed of Crosby's role.[125] A bail delay of about week was used to protect Crosby's identity. It was during this time that he also learned of his new employer, the Committee for Detecting Conspiracies.[126] The legend of Enoch Crosby had begun.

His first covert mission involved infiltrating a neighborhood of Loyalists, who, like his previous target, planned to raise a company for the British army. Using his skills at assimilation, Crosby infiltrated the group, even living for a time in a mountain cave with Captain James Robinson, the English officer who would command the newly formed group, as he collected information and then discreetly passed it to authorities. The entire company of men, including Captain Robinson, was captured and made prisoners.

The monument over the grave of Enoch Crosby inside Gilead Cemetery in Carmel, New York.

Crosby then returned to shoemaking—his cover. About ten days passed before his next assignment could be delivered: he was to go to Bennington, Vermont, and then continue westerly to a place called Walloomsac. There he was to call on one Hazard Wilcox, a Tory of much notoriety, and ascertain if anything was going on there injurious to the American cause. Again, Crosby thwarted an attempt to raise an enemy company.[127]

After two subsequent missions in Albany County and Poughkeepsie, which yielded little result, Crosby returned home with the approbation of the committee, believed to have been in late May 1777.[128] Two additional stints followed in May 1779 and May 1780. During his last stint, men in his company made their way to New Jersey, where they remained until late fall. During that campaign, Major André was arrested, condemned and executed. Several company soldiers witnessed the execution but not Crosby, as he was sergeant of the guard that day.

ADDENDUM

Crosby was supervisor of the town of Southeast from 1812 to 1813 and also served as justice of the peace for many years.[129]

The inscription of Enoch Crosby's gravestone in Gilead Cemetery reads, "To the Memory of ENOCH CROSBY ('Harvey Birch'), Patriot Spy of the American Revolution, June 5, 1750–June 26, 1835 [space] He Braved Danger and Death That This Land Might Be Free to the Cause of Liberty He Offered His All. Without Hope of Reward. Honored by Washington. Revered by His Countrymen. We Who Inherit the Freedom for Which He Toiled Raise This Monument to His Glorious Memory." A historical marker with similar information also rests on the west side of Route 6 in Southeast, New York, in between Drewville Road and Route 312, across from the reservoir.

Chapter 11

Nathan Hale

And because that boy said those words, and because he died, thousands of other young men have given their lives to his country.
—Dr. Edward Everett Hale, great-nephew of Nathan Hale, at the dedication of the Hale statue in New York, 1893

"Swing the rebel off," ordered the provost marshal.[130] In a blink of an eye, Hale's body lunged forward—the very instant that separates angels from men—then snapped back sharply; only the noose separated him from his last step on earth (some place that step on top of his own coffin, above his very grave). For three days in the September heat, Nathan Hale's body hung lifeless and in decay. As an allegory of association it was ridiculed (A British letter claims a sign—reading George Washington—was even placed to Hale's chest like a bulletin board) and spat upon until finally a slave saw to its liberation. Removed and buried unclothed, the body was interred without prayer, without marker and without implication, or so it was thought.

THE MISSION

Turning to the Continental Congress on September 6, 1776, Washington affirmed, "Their designs [British ships] we cannot learn, nor have we been able to procure the least information lately, of any of their plans or intended operations."[131] Without possession of Long Island, he believed, New York could not be held; his army had been scattered about York Island

Captain Nathan Hale was executed as spy by the British on September 22, 1776. *LC-USZ62-48286.*

and could not endure another defeat such as at Brooklyn. The seemingly endless consternation weighed heavily on a commander in chief still unable to make up his mind regarding occupation. Meanwhile, the Tories were well positioned, holding two-thirds of the city. Following council, Washington summoned Colonel Thomas Knowlton.

The Connecticut commander, who hugged the rail at Bunker Hill and led the night attack at Charlestown, would now be given the task of intelligence gathering. Certainly he, if anyone, could find a man among his elite squad to accept such a mission: to maneuver behind enemy lines, accurately access their position and then safely return. Initially, Knowlton's request was met with silence, the perils of the mission clearly understood. Later, a rhetorical comment from a noncommissioned French officer put it into perspective: "I am willing to be shot, but not to be hung."[132]

Although Hale had taken part in the Siege of Boston and now led one of four companies in Knowlton's Rangers, he was frustrated that he had rendered no real service to his country.[133] The youngest of the commanding officer's captains then stated, "I will undertake it."[134] To acquire such desperately needed details, Hale thought, was the perfect opportunity for distinction. "I wish to be useful," he would declare, "and every kind of service necessary to the public good becomes honorable by being necessary."[135]

A fellow Connecticut officer, Captain William Hull attempted to be honest with his college friend: Hale was, by nature, "too frank and open for deceit and disguise," he asserted.[136] He also forewarned his compatriot that the character of a spy was not respected in the eyes of most but rather repulsed. From a confidant, they were cutting remarks. Hull then insisted "that for the love of country, for the love of kindred, to abandon an enterprise which would only end in the sacrifice of the dearest interests of both."[137] Hale paused, then looked into the eyes of his fellow countryman and uttered, "I will reflect, and do nothing but what duty demands."[138] He then disappeared into the night.

Days later, from Harlem Heights, Hale embarked on his perilous mission. Now in the company of Sergeant Stephen Hampstead and Asher Wright, the group would take the safest route east to the shoreline, where they would then look for a place to navigate Long Island Sound. That proved to be Norwalk, Connecticut. Before his departure across the estuary, Hale entrusted Hempstead with his private papers and silver shoe buckles.[139]

Dressed in civilian's clothes, the guise of a Dutch schoolmaster desirous of work, Hale stepped aboard the sloop *Schuyler* for the next leg of his journey. Under command of Captain Charles Pond, the ship headed toward a landing near Huntington. Upon landing, knowledge of his actions would cease.

After more than a week in enemy-held territory, the military situation had changed. The Americans had been pushed back to where 127th Street now stands, and whatever provisions Hale had made before his departure were at risk.

"Mistakingly, he signaled an English warship (while awaiting a small craft for his safe return) and was seized. When searched, his notes compromised him at once; taken on board the frigate he was sent back to New York," according to Edward Everett Hale, the orator and political leader, whose father was the nephew of Nathan Hale.

His capture, as others believe, may have come through his own naïvety.[140] Perhaps he unwisely confided the truth to a stranger or was even recognized by a friend or relative, as indicated by the Consider Tiffany manuscript—a Tory storekeeper's version of the American Revolution—in the Library of Congress. Noted historian David McCullough, who mentions the Patriot in his landmark work 1776, believes the mission was "doomed from the start" and that Hale was a "poor choice" for numerous reasons.[141]

Upon apprehension, Hale was taken before General William Howe at his headquarters in the Beekman House, a rural part of modern-day Manhattan at Fifty-first Street and First Avenue. The information found in Hale's possession sealed his fate; Howe had no doubt of his intentions. An unyielding Hale stood without prevarication. Minus trial, Howe gave orders for his execution the following morning and placed him into the hands of the provost marshal. Deeply religious, Hale requested the presence of clergy and a Bible. Both appeals were denied.

THE EXECUTION

Provost Marshal William Cunningham may have been one of the most vile men to walk the face of the earth. Boasting often that he had caused the death of two thousand American soldiers, the cowardly murderer was known to have starved prisoners to death aboard the prison ships anchored in New York harbor by depriving them of their rations, which he would confiscate then sell and pocket the money. His role, as he saw it, was public humiliation. Delayed on this day, by a fire that had spread throughout the city, it was late in the forenoon—about 11:00 a.m.—before Hale's execution could commence.

It was under the flag of truce that Captain William Hull received this information, according to his memoirs, from Captain John Montresor, then on the staff of General William Howe: "On the morning of his execution, my station being near the fatal spot, and I [John Montresor] requested the provost marshal to permit the prisoner to sit in my marquee while he was making the necessary preparations. Captain Hale entered; he was calm, and bore himself with gentle dignity."[142] Hale then asked for writing materials, which Montresor furnished him, and wrote two letters.[143] He was shortly summoned to the gallows.

THE WORDS AND LOCATION

It was William Hull who would report Montresor's account of Hale's last words: "I only regret that I have but one life to lose for my country."[144] Those now-famous words are a twist from a line in Joseph Addison's tragedy Cato. With no official records, it's possible that these words differed or were part of a larger passage or speech. Nathan Hale was hanged on the morning of September 22, 1776, in a park near the Beekman House, not far from the East River. The exact location of his hanging has also been questioned. Hale's capture and execution were, however, noted in the diary of General William Howe. He made this entry on September 22, 1776: "A spy from the enemy by his own full confession, apprehended last night, was executed [this] day at 11 o'clock in front of the Artillery Park."

THE MAN

Born on June 6, 1755, in Coventry, Connecticut, Nathan was the son of Richard Hale and Elizabeth Strong. Elizabeth would die at a young age but not before having an enormous effect on her sixth child. To the Hales, faith and education were paramount, followed closely by family chores. Two years after the death of his mother, a fourteen-year-old Nathan entered college at Yale, where he was accompanied by his brother Enoch.

Inside his walls in New Haven, Nathan thrived; his high scholarship and gift for athleticism endeared him to many. Now a handsome young man, tall and muscular, his good looks were enhanced by blue eyes and light reddish-brown hair. If his looks failed to attract attention—which was unlikely—his charm certainly would. On graduation day, he stood proudly among the first thirteen in a class of thirty-six.

College days behind him, he turned to teaching, first in East Haddam (fall 1773 until spring 1774) and then followed by a stint in New London (late spring 1774 to summer 1775). "I love my employment; find many friends among strangers," he said. "I have a school of more than thirty boys to instruct, about half of them in Latin; and my salary is satisfactory."[145] At a time when the opposite sex might have been passed over, Hale didn't give it a thought, saying, "During the summer I had a morning class for young ladies—about a score—from five to seven o'clock."[146] When the Lexington alarm sounded, he, too, had to make a choice: "I have thought much of

Nathan Hale Schoolhouse, Nathan Hale Park in East Haddam, Middlesex County. *HABS CONN,4-HADE,2—1.*

never quitting it but with life, but at present there seems an opportunity for more extended service."[147]

Lieutenant Hale was attached to the Seventh Connecticut Regiment under the command of Colonel Charles Webb, and in late September 1775, they departed for Cambridge. It was there that he would engage the enemy and motivate his comrades. During a difficult and lasting struggle, his adversary was finally driven out of the city; for his valor in the heat of battle, Hale was commissioned a captain in January 1776.[148] On December 23, 1775, following extended duty, Hale took leave back to Connecticut, and while details are vague, he returned to camp the last week in January 1776. His regiment departed Roxbury only a few days after the British evacuation.

THE LEGACY

As the protagonist of the Revolution, he had distanced himself from the summer soldier, or the sunshine Loyalist, who shrinks so conveniently

As a martyr spy of the American Revolution, Nathan Hale is the heart and soul of every Connecticut veteran. Statue by sculptor Larry Wasiele for the Town of Coventry, Connecticut.

from the service to his country.[149] He stood proudly. When his enemy gave no quarter, he did not ask. Icons of freedom do not plead, nor do they lament.

The ramifications of Hale's death were not immediate; history answers to no interval. His place in the pantheon of American history would be secured later, thanks to the efforts of many, including Connecticut lawyer George Dudley Seymour.

If the tree of liberty must be watered with the blood of Patriots, as Thomas Jefferson believed, then no more a Patriot could be found than Nathan Hale.

POSTLUDE

Since the body of Nathan Hale was never found, his family erected a cenotaph above an empty grave in Nathan Hale Cemetery in Coventry, Connecticut.

Perhaps no man has been more memorialized in the state of Connecticut than Nathan Hale. His name has been attached to battalions; chapters of the Daughters of the American Revolution (Nathan Hale Chapter, Minnesota, and Nathan Hale Memorial Chapter, Connecticut); dormitories at the University of Connecticut and Phillips Academy; fife and drum corps; a fort (Fort Nathan Hale, New Haven); schools in Coventry, East Haddam, Enfield, Manchester, Meriden, New Haven and Norwalk; statues in Coventry and New Haven; and even a submarine, USS *Nathan Hale* (SSBN-623). Nathan Hale was named "Connecticut State Hero" by an act of the Connecticut General Assembly on October 1, 1985.

The Nathan Hale Homestead, located at 2299 South Street in Coventry, Connecticut, is a lasting tribute to the Hale family. The impressive home was owned by Nathan's father, Deacon Richard Hale.

IV. TALLMADGE'S LATTICE

Chapter 12

The Culper Ring

By playing at Chess then, we may learn: 1ˢᵗ, Foresight, which looks a little into futurity, and considers the consequences that may attend an action…2ⁿᵈ, Circumspection, which surveys the whole Chess-board, or scene of action:—the relation of the several Pieces, and their situations;…3ʳᵈ, Caution, not to make our moves too hastily.
—*Benjamin Franklin, "The Morals of Chess" (1750)*

For five arduous years (1778–83), and perhaps months beyond, the Culper Spy Ring operated in and around New York City, the site of British headquarters. Covert, competent and concise, the goal of this Patriot intelligence network was the successful delivery of information to and from General George Washington. Members of this ring were not the only spies assuming this task, nor the only network, but they were the most intriguing.

OF VALUE AND VINDICATION

New York City was a high-value target, an objective that the British command deemed imperative to its mission. Although both combatants had placed a premium on controlling the Hudson River, a strategic watercourse, to General George Washington, its significance was unmatched. Ever since his defeat at Fort Washington, near the north end of Manhattan Island, he had become obsessed with vindication.

On Saturday, November 16, 1776, the capitulation of Fort Washington proved nothing short of devastating, with many historians deeming it a calamity. Standing on the rocky terrain opposite Fort Lee, on the New Jersey side of the Hudson River, George Washington witnessed the annihilation through his own telescope as body after body of his soldiers were bayoneted by General Howe's men.[150] As the warriors fell, so, too, did the self-esteem of an American general. Just how, and when, to retrieve his pride remained the conundrum.

1778

In the spring of 1778, the British still rested comfortably in New York City at Manhattan Island, then extending only a dozen or so blocks up from the Battery. In June, preparation for a possible French assault found Sir Henry Clinton—having been ordered to evacuate Philadelphia—marching to New York to reinforce the garrison. Dispersed across the islands— Manhattan, Staten and Long—the bolstered British army, safeguarded by water, appeared impregnable; only one sentineled aqueduct linked the island trio: that of Kingsbridge, which spanned the Harlem River, coupling the upper end of Manhattan with Lower Westchester County.

As inviolable as the objective appeared, Washington knew it was not invincible, at least not to deception, as proven by the efforts of Colonel Elias Dayton's spy network operating between Staten Island and New Jersey. A surveillance labyrinth, he thought, composed of both operatives and networks, the ne plus ultra. More than a year earlier, while headquartered in Morristown, Washington had appointed Nathaniel Sackett to

Benjamin Tallmadge, the architect of the Culper Ring. *LC-USZ62-59149.*

obtain enemy information.[151] As an experienced spy hunter, Sackett had been a member of the New York Committee for Detecting and Defeating Conspiracies. Reporting directly to Washington, he was a logical choice.

Months passed, however, and expectations were not being met. In late 1778, to replace departing brigadier general Charles Scott, Washington appointed a new director of military intelligence, Benjamin Tallmadge, captain of the Second Continental Dragoons and Sackett's military contact. The creation of an additional espionage nexus in and around the British stronghold would be his major objective.

With New York as his chess board, sound information would allow Washington to make the perfect move. He was playing against the very best, and he knew it.

TALLMADGE'S LATTICE

Operating primarily out of Setauket, New York City and Fairfield, Tallmadge's network was dependent on logistics—its complexity was precisely why it would be improbable to the enemy.

Setauket, Long Island, New York

Why Setauket? It had an associated comfort level. Washington's new director was born there on February 25, 1754. The son of Presbyterian minister Benjamin Tallmadge and Susannah Smith, he spent his childhood days on the North Shore of modern-day Long Island before heading off to New Haven, Connecticut, and the walls of Yale University. Graduating in 1773, Tallmadge, a friend of Nathan Hale, shared his classmate's ambitions; he, too, became a Connecticut teacher and entered the army following the Lexington alarm.[152] Commissioned as a lieutenant on June 20, 1776, Tallmadge served in Colonel John Chester's regiment of Wadsworth's Connecticut Brigade and eventually rose up the ladder to become brigade major, followed by captain of the Dragoons.

Far from a surveillance expert, the Yale alum was nonetheless passionate over his designation (the extent of that enthusiasm attributable to the possible vindication of Hale's hanging has often been pondered) and undeniably committed. The attentive director struck a powerful pose and delivered his orders with pride and precision. As his commander had entrusted him, so, too, Tallmadge entrusted his selections.

Abraham Woodhull, a boyhood friend, became an early Tallmadge recruit. A farmer by trade, Woodhull would assume the day-to-day operations on Long Island. Undertaking dangerous reconnaissance and even recruitment missions into the city, Woodhull displayed tremendous fortitude. The more than fifty-mile excursion was fraught with danger; if the hoodlums he encountered didn't kill him, he thought, certainly the adverse conditions would. Hostile foraging skirmishes were as common as rut-strewn roads and broken wagon wheels. For protection—and there was never enough for the anxiety-filled farmer whose relative General Nathaniel Woodhull was killed by the British—Woodhull assumed the moniker "Samuel Culper Sr.," thus the sobriquet for the operation. Tallmadge, too, took a new designation: "John Bolton."

From his Setauket hub, Woodhull would constantly appraise information—in his estimation, there were no routine missives. The journey across Long Island Sound to Fairfield, Connecticut, and then into the hands of a New York– or New Jersey–based General Washington was fraught with uncertainty, resource dependent and typically a week in length.[153]

Traversing the channel was left in the capable hands of Caleb Brewster. Ironically, while a veteran soldier, his task throughout the war was to command a fleet of whaleboats operating out of Connecticut; disrupting British and Tory shipping on Long Island Sound became their trademark. The bold and brusque mariner was also no stranger to Tallmadge, having served under him at the capture of Fort St. George at Mastic, New York, in November 1780.

Austin Roe, a tavern owner in East Setauket, also worked with the Culper Ring; his occupation, with its regular need for supplies, was a dependable cover. Making the weekly trek into New York, Roe would conveniently add fresh dispatches alongside his produce—one of his suppliers just happened to be Robert Townsend. Upon his arrival home, Roe would then place the notes in a box buried on Woodhull's farm. Called a "dead drop," the method avoided face-to-face contact.

Assisting in the process was Woodhull's neighbor Anna Smith Strong, who reportedly used the laundry on her clothesline to leave signals regarding Brewster's whereabouts for Woodhull and who coincidentally lived up to her surname. Anna was married to Patriot justice Selah Strong, who was presumed to be a spy and confined aboard the British prison ship *Jersey*.[154]

The Setauket nerve center in place, it was time to establish their city contacts.

New York City

The key to New York City would be the well-educated merchant Robert Townsend, or "Samuel Culper Jr.," as he would become known. His cover as, among other things, a wholesaler allowed him to travel to places like his hometown of Oyster Bay without rousing suspicion. Townsend also published stories in the *Royal Gazette*, a pro-Tory newspaper printed by James Rivington. Since the Patriots detested Rivington, certainly Townsend, he thought, would not fare much better. (Documents revealed in 1959 proved that Rivington was an American operative, more likely a double agent.)[155] It would be from a coffeehouse—under the watchful eye of Rivington, its operator—that Townsend would gather useful information. As British officers gossiped over a cup of java, not only did liquid spill but so did secrets. One of the regular officers—a would-be poet whose work found its way into the *Gazette* as well as into secret dispatches—was Major John André, the chief British intelligence officer in New York.

Not all is known of the additional agents feeding this intelligence pipeline, but what was certain was that Townsend was the ringleader, the principal contact from 1778 to 1783.

Fairfield, Connecticut

Handling affairs in Connecticut would be Tallmadge himself; if he was not in Fairfield to receive the messages personally, he would appoint another officer—who would understand the urgency of the delivery but not the identity of the source—to meet with Brewster.[156] Post riders were then dispatched to Washington's headquarters.

A sample journey might begin in New York, where Townsend overhears that three thousand reinforcements are due into port at the end of the month. Choosing to use his copy of Tallmadge's codebook (see pages 126–28), he ciphers a message, possibly in invisible ink, to paper. This message is then hidden in part of Austin Roe's weekly tavern supplies bound for Setauket. Once home, Roe sets out for Woodhull's farm to complete a "dead drop." Picking up the drop at his convenience, Woodhull undertakes a deciphering procedure to determine the message and its importance; had Woodhull been visiting the city, he might have been told the information. Deciding to pass it along, Woodhull then gives the message to Brewster, who takes it twelve miles across the sound. There,

The Culper Ring Message Highway is believed to have traveled from New York City to Setauket, New York, over to Fairfield, Connecticut, and then on to Washington's headquarters.

Tallmadge completes the same process as Woodhull. Sensing its urgency, he then dispatches the quickest riders available to deliver the message to the General's Camp. Upon arrival, Alexander Hamilton, a Washington aide, unveils the message—with or without solution—by deciphering the missive using the same codebook. Days having now passed, Washington, too, must determine what, if any, course of action to take.

THE TALLMADGE CODEBOOK

No more than four copies of Tallmadge's secret writing system, a method that he invented, were distributed. He kept one and gave one each to Townsend, Washington and Woodhull. Certainly, the limited distribution and its uniqueness contributed to its success; he substituted numbers for words, and words that

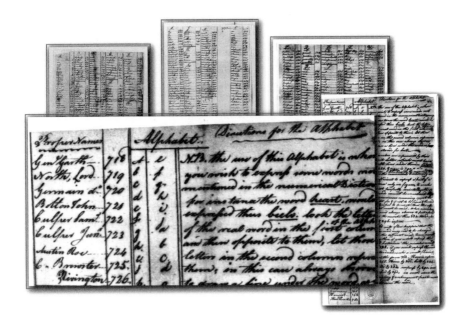

Actual pages from Washington's copy of the Tallmadge codebook. An enlargement from the top of one of those pages lists some familiar proper names. *GWP-LC-S4-I25; 1741-1799: Series 4. General Correspondence.*

did not have a number used a cipher, the exception being simple words, such as prepositions, that would not hint to its content. The messages were not extremely difficult to decipher, if, of course, you had the codebook.

For further security, Tallmadge also assigned numeric identities: John Bolton was 721; Caleb Brewster, 725; Samuel Culper Sr., 722; Samuel Culper Jr., 723; Austin Roe, 724; and George Washington, 711, along with a few others. (Note: There have been references to an Agent 355 working out of New York, but her existence remains unsubstantiated. Some historians speculate the "355" is regarding the number inside Tallmadge's codebook that means lady.)

Agents were cautious not to use another person's real name. For that process, Tallmadge provided an alphabet cipher:

Line 1: a b c d e f g h i j k l m n o p q r s t u v w x y z
Line 2: e f g h i j a b c d o m n p q r k l u v w x y z s t

For example, the name of author Thomas Paine would translate to: vbqneu recpi. A cipher was also provided for the digits zero through nine, which were also represented by the letters: e, f, g, i, k, m, n, o, q and u. To differentiate the letters, Tallmadge had a double line placed underneath them.

Frequently, dispatches were written in invisible ink, called a "sympathetic" stain. After 1779, this ink was often of a variety developed by British doctor and chemist Sir James Jay, brother of Patriot leader John Jay, the benefit being that Jay's ink, unlike others, did not become visible by heating. It was a two-bottle system that required one chemical for writing (agent) and another for revealing (reagent); as a precaution, the developer was never given to any of the spies. Washington himself encouraged certain resourceful yet deceptive techniques, such as writing the information on the blank leaves of pamphlets or common books or even on the blank leaves at each end of registers, almanacs or books of small value.

Washington's Moles

If Washington had learned anything from his experience with espionage, it was the value of alternative sources. He would not restrict himself to one agent or network.[157] A good example of this method can be found in Hercules Mulligan, whom Washington personally utilized.[158] As a Kings College–educated tailor, Mulligan often accumulated information from the stylish British officers being fitted in his Wall Street shop. Emigrating at the age of six, Mulligan grew into a likable Irishman who could "sling the blarney with the best of 'em." When intelligence flowed freely from his British patrons, Mulligan, also a member of the Sons of Liberty, saw to it that Washington got a copy; just how, nobody seems to know, but reportedly he exposed two plots—the first in the winter of 1779 and another two years later—to kill the American leader.

Also, in February 1778, Mulligan's brother Hugh, a successful trader, learned of three hundred horse soldiers being dispatched to New London, Connecticut, to intercept Washington, who was traveling to Newport to meet with French general Rochambeau. Hugh passed the information on to Hercules, who then relayed it to Washington's camp. The general soon altered his Rhode Island route.

THE ART OF THE MASTERS

Assimilation, as both Washington and Tallmadge saw it, was critical to success; if the agents could live undetected among the enemy, in roles conducive to intelligence, they could be successful. Nonetheless, Washington also wanted a degree of separation from the spy ring; only Tallmadge had direct contact. This level of detachment would allow him to conduct his own private operations. By cross-checking his sources—his own networks against those he personally employed—Washington improved his odds of success. It was his own best advice: trust but verify.

EPILOGUE

The Culper Ring was an impressive display of American espionage in its infancy, Washington's *coup d'œil militaire*. Ordinary individuals—not highly trained operatives—were conducting extraordinary tasks and dangerous deeds.[159] Although alerted to the intelligence network, even suspecting Brewster, the British failed to infiltrate or suspend the matrix.[160] When you consider that the system operated in New York City, a tempestuous intelligence domain, and didn't become public knowledge until the twentieth century, it's clear you have nothing short of a masterful accomplishment.

They transmitted information about arrivals and departures, casualty figures, locations, movements, names and supply levels of the enemy. Of notable acts, we have everything from forwarding information regarding British attempts at counterfeiting American currency—the enemy in possession of identical paper—to stonewalling Clinton's plan to disrupt the French arrival at Newport; the extent to which the group assisted with the apprehension of the British spy John André might also be added. These were actions of immeasurable value that only Washington himself could assess.

For its role, Connecticut could not have stood prouder. Of the ring, none shines brighter than its impresario, Benjamin Tallmadge, an extraordinary man—Patriot, politician and educator—who remained ever so humble. After the war, Tallmadge (1754–1835) married Mary, one of the daughters of signer William Floyd, and settled in Litchfield. Serving his community in a variety of roles, including as postmaster and as a member of the United States House of Representatives, Tallmadge died a respected man. He is interred in East Cemetery in town.

The Tallmadge family plot in East Cemetery in Litchfield, Connecticut.

Always at home in the very small village of Setauket, Abraham Woodhull (1750–1826), remained there after the war. He married twice, served as Suffolk County justice and died in the place he loved. Woodhull's grave in the Setauket Presbyterian Church graveyard was marked by the Mayflower Chapter of the Daughters of the Revolution in 1936.

Robert Townsend (1753–1838) departed New York City after the war for the comfort of Oyster Bay. There he managed the estate of his father, Samuel Townsend, before drifting into relative obscurity, his memory later resurrected by a determined Long Island historian.[161]

As for Austin Roe (1748–1830), he moved to Patchogue in 1798, founded Roe's Hotel and died there at the age of eighty-one.[162]

Originally from Setauket, Caleb Brewster (1747–1827) moved to the Black Rock section of Bridgeport (then part of Fairfield), Connecticut. Pensioned by Congress for his war efforts, he captained a revenue cutter for years. If there was a smuggler in the area, Brewster could find him.

At war's end, Anna Smith (Nancy) Strong (1740–1812), whose home had the perfect vista of the sound, reunited with her family in Setauket.

The story of Agent 355 begins, and perhaps ends, with only one direct reference from Abraham Woodhull in a 1778 letter to General George Washington.[163] As an undying citation, it seems to have no rival; I will personally let her rest upon a grassy knoll.

THE INTELLIGENCE STATE

As we close the book on the Culper Ring, we also proudly validate our claim to being the "Intelligence State." Clearly, covert intelligence played a critical role in the American Revolution, a majority precipitated by Spies of Revolutionary Connecticut, from Benedict Arnold to Nathan Hale.

Notes

Preface

1. Inspired by the words of John Dickinson, Thomas Jefferson, Patrick Henry and John Adams.

Introduction

2. The signing of the document began on August 2, but several men—Elbridge Gerry, Oliver Wolcott, Lewis Morris, Thomas McKean and Matthew Thornton—signed at a later date. (Two others, John Dickinson and Robert R. Livingston, never signed at all.) No formal signing ceremony ever took place. The painting was commissioned in 1817.
3. Adams to John Trumbull, March 13, 1817, Massachusetts Historical Society.
4. *Autobiography, Reminiscences and Letters of John Trumbull, from 1756 to 1841* (New York & London: Wiley and Putnum, 1841).
5. Ibid. Stuart was being tutored by West.
6. *Trumbull Autobiography*.
7. Ibid. The police warrant that mentioned Trumbull had additional instruction from undersecretary Sir Benjamin Thompson, himself an American Loyalist.

8. Ibid. Artist Benjamin West and John Singleton Copley became Trumbull's sureties in a bond for two hundred pounds.

9. Ibid.

10. Trumbull glossed over both his artwork and questions regarding his imprisonment as a spy.

CHAPTER 1

11. Literacy rates were the highest in the New England colonies; about 75 percent of males and 65 percent of females could read, according to the 1750 estimate.

12. Named after the combatants in the respective theaters, it was also known as the Seven Years' War.

13. All were unsuccessful punitive measures aimed at reversing the trend of colonial resistance to parliamentary authority. Bear in mind that this was months before Lexington. See Suffolk Resolves.

14. "The Diary of John Adams," from Adams Family Papers, Massachusetts Historical Society.

15. Wain, *Signers of the Declaration of Independence.*

16. Sherman was also behind the Connecticut Compromise, reiterating need for bicameral legislation.

17. The long "s" [f] was used in the vast majority of books published in English during the seventeenth and eighteenth centuries and dates back at least to the Middle Ages.

18. It wasn't until armed conflict began that the majority of colonists sought outright independence. Loyalists were those who supported King George III, though those colonists who were Patriots called their adversaries Tories. The British planned to seize the weapons cache stored in Concord and arrest Samuel Adams and John Hancock, who were staying in Lexington.

19. Following the engagement, he preceded General George Washington into New York and the blighted Battle of Long Island in August 1776. It took a paralytic stroke to finally force Putnam into retirement.

20. "Connecticut in the American Revolution," an exhibition from the Library and Museum Collections of the Society of the Cincinnati, Anderson House, Washington, D.C., October 27, 2001–May 11, 2002. Selden heard the call in 1775 and died on October 11, 1776.

21. See Connecticut author Kevin Phillips's masterful work, *1775, A Good Year for Revolution*, published by Viking, New York (2012), for a thorough understanding.
22. See Chapter 4: "Silas Deane."
23. Over two hundred privateers roamed the waters in search of British supply boats. Many originated from the West Indies.
24. Trumbull, *Governor of Connecticut, 1769–1784*.
25. Ibid.
26. Ibid.
27. By year's end (1776), Washington was in need of a permanent standing army, adequately supplied and with a way to counteract disease, especially smallpox. Connecticut would assist him in making these changes.
28. A psychological victory, such as Trenton or Princeton—both intelligence-driven—could, as Washington thought, boost morale and benefit reenlistment.

Chapter 2

29. Braddock died of wounds suffered during an ambush that may have been avoided by quality intelligence. It is fascinating how Washington preserves his honor despite his copious need for surveillance.
30. Letter from Washington to Robert Hunter Morris, January 5, 1766, in *The Writings of George Washington, Vol I*. (Washington, D.C.: U.S. Government Printing Office, 1931–44), 268.
31. Feel free to add a mix of revenge and compensation as well. The glorification of espionage in popular culture reflects how America has evolved.
32. Many intelligence agencies require similar qualities. Visit associated websites such as those of the Central Intelligence Agency, Federal Bureau of Investigation and others for more information.
33. See "Spy Letters of the American Revolution," From the collection of the Clements Library, University of Michigan. Letter from Thompson to Gage, May 6, 1775. It has been suspected that Benjamin Church, who was tried for treason by Washington, may also have been involved with Thompson.
34. It was a substitution code based on a prose passage of 682 characters. See "Codes and Ciphers," in "Intelligence Techniques," Central Intelligence Agency website; John Adams and Benjamin Franklin were also noteworthy ciphers and proponents of invisible ink.

35. This technique provided more security than a simple (mono-alphabetic) substitution cipher.

36. *Entick's Spelling Dictionary*, in a later edition, is available on-line through Google books. A "book code" uses three numbers to make a word: the page number of the book, then the line on that page, followed by the word on that line, counting from the left. For example: 86.2.5 refers the reader to page 86, line 2, word 5.

37. See "Spy Letters of the American Revolution," from the collection of the Clements Library, University of Michigan, for some outstanding examples. Paper was scarce and handmade.

38. Sir Henry Clinton used this technique. See letter from Clinton to Burgoyne, August 10, 1777, in the Clinton manuscripts at the Clements Library, University of Michigan.

39. British spies did an excellent job at concealing their messages. A fine example is a miniature letter from Howe to Burgoyne, July 17, 1777, which was hidden inside a quill. See "Spy Letters of the American Revolution," collection of the Clements Library, University of Michigan.

40. George Washington's expense account is available through the Library of Congress. During the American Revolutionary War, Washington is believed to have spent more than 10 percent of his military funds on intelligence. Two additional sample entries in support include entry 111 on April 1, 1776, which reads: "To amount of Sundry Inst[ances] per Mem[orandum] for Secret Services to the date…$5, 232," and entry three on January 1, 1777, which reads: "To Secret Services since the Army left Cambridge in April—while it lay at New York and during its retreat as above…$8,414."

41. Boudinot, *Life of Elias Boudinot*. New York.

CHAPTER 3

42. Corresponding with the enemy in cipher, Church shared military secrets when Americans were not yet fixed on independence. Only later would files reveal the tremendous depth of information provided to the British. Elbridge Gerry, Elisha Porter and Reverend Samuel West decrypted the implicating letter.

43. Along with spies, local informants, such as merchants or scouts, were also used. These individuals, many with direct access to information, proved extraordinarily useful.

44. Aitken has struck many as a radical dissident turned spy simply to justify, at least in his own mind, his behavior. He admitted the destruction to a British agent who was posing as an imprisoned American.

45. Stiles, *History and Genealogies of Ancient Windsor*. It begins on page 336, under the title "The History of Daniel Bissell the Spy."

46. This was sworn public testimony on January 7, 1818, in Richmond, Ontario County, State of New York before Wm. Baker, Justice of the Peace. Records available through the NARA.

47. Stiles, *History and Genealogies of Ancient Windsor*. Arnold had returned to New York during the summer and was authorized by Clinton to raid the port of New London in September. His new British role was of paramount concern to Washington.

48. Ibid.

49. Ibid.

50. Found at www.purpleheart.org. Bissell died on August 21, 1824.

51. Clark was aide-de-camp to Major General Nathanael Greene. Through Clark, Washington created false intelligence that led Howe to believe Horatio Gates, victor of Saratoga, was marching to his doorstep.

52. Finally settling in Brockville, Leeds County, Ontario, Canada, Solomon Johns died at the young age of thirty-five.

53. Nehemiah Marks (1746–1799). See the Clements Library, University of Michigan for additional information.

54. This is according to military records in the possession of Dr. Henry Eno. See also www.rootsweb.ancestry.com.

55. Randall, *Ethan Allen*. Before this dispatch, Phelps had eavesdropped on a British conversation inside a farmhouse. Hickok also served with distinction during the Revolution.

56. Ibid. Naturally, the British garrison inside the fort was not in fear of attack because it was forbidden. Besides the confiscation of valuable ordnance and supplies, the Americans now had a load of prisoners bound for a Hartford jail.

57. Noah Phelps died in Simsbury on November 4, 1809. On his tombstone in Simsbury Cemetery is inscribed: "A Patriot of 1776. To such we are indebted for our Independence."

58. Outside the state, many known or suspected spies have surfaced over the years, including Elias Boudinot (New Jersey), James Bowdoin II (Boston), Alexander Clough (New Jersey), Lewis Costigin (New York), Lydia Darragh (Philadelphia), Elias Dayton (New Jersey), David Gray (New York), Nancy Morgan Hart (Georgia), George Higday (New York), John

Honeyman (New Jersey), Elijah Hunter (New York), Dominique L'Eclise (Canada), Allan McLane (Philadelphia) and Abraham Patten (New York).

CHAPTER 4

59. Communicated through James Lovell, the letter was dated December 8, 1777. Adams succeeded Deane on November 28, 1777, through a congressional appointment.

60. Joseph Webb, a Deane client, was a successful mercantilist.

61. Instructions to Deane from the Naval Committee, at the New York Historical Society. On November 17, 1775, Deane received a letter from the Naval Committee of Congress, chaired by John Adams. It requested his assistance to make worthy two military vessels. This an example of the trust Deane had earned from his peers.

62. Deane was given a lengthy set of instructions from the committee dated March 3, 1776, from Philadelphia. The document can be found in the Connecticut Historical Society Museum.

63. Deane to Committee of Correspondence, August 16, 1776. Deane used a heat-developing invisible ink consisting of cobalt chloride, glycerine and water. Later, he would turn to Dr. Jay's recipe. Deane's Paris welcome included visits from Julien-Alexander Achard de Bonvouloir; George Lupton (Jacobus van Zandt), a British agent; and James Aitken.

64. Beaumarchais had experience conducting secret diplomatic missions. In September 1775, Charles Gravier, comte de Vergennes, had sent Achard de Bonvouloir, a secret agent to America to assess the seriousness of the American frustration. To maintain an appearance of neutrality while providing the rebels with secret arms and funds would become the French position through Roderiquez, Hortalez and Company, which traded supplies for commodities, such as tobacco. Both Spain and private investors also had a stake in the venture. Congress still owes Beaumarchais 3,600,000 livres.

65. The committee announced that Thomas Jefferson declined to go to France and that Arthur Lee of London would be appointed. In his London capacity, Lee was the first enlisted agent by the Committee of Secret Correspondence.

66. The Lees would have profited directly from the sale of tobacco in exchange for arms. See Paul's brilliant work *Unlikely Allies*.

67. Lee was close friends with the artful British spy Paul Wentworth (See "Edward Bancroft"). Later, it was discovered that Lee's personal secretary, Major John Thornton, was working for the British.

68. McCullough, *John Adams*, 196. Lacking accurate records, the hearing degenerated into personal bickering even leading to the resignation of Henry Laurens (a Deane opponent) as president of Congress. He was replaced by John Jay. Noted historian David McCullough, in his masterful 2001 work *John Adams*, concluded that Deane "let himself be bought."

69. The letters were published from October 24, 1781, until December 12, 1781, the last being addressed to Benjamin Tallmadge. An essay from Deane was also published in December. (See Chapter 12: "The Culper Ring.")

70. The manuscript copy of the address was sent to America by Deane's son, with a request, dated November 3, 1783, that his brother Barnabas should have it printed. That was done in Hartford by Hudson & Goodwin.

Chapter 5

71. Goodrich, *Curiosities of Human Nature.*

72. Allen was acting on intelligence that Benedict Arnold had provided Colonel Samuel H. Parsons.

73. Allen, *Narrative of Captivity.*

74. Ibid. Although these are Allen's words, they have been challenged by other accounts.

75. Botkin, *Treasury of New England Folklore.* British accounts of the action differed.

76. Allen's true age has forever been questioned; Allen's later writings were influenced by deism.

Chapter 6

77. "Statue of Colonel Thomas Knowlton, Ceremonies at the Unveiling."

78. Sons of the American Revolution, Connecticut, "Lt. Col. Thomas Knowlton, Connecticut's Forgotten Hero."

79. "Statue of Colonel Thomas Knowlton, Ceremonies at the Unveiling."
80. Only 20 individuals from Israel Putnam's company would return home from Havana, though he began with 107 men. Knowlton also took part in the siege and fall of Ticonderoga in July 1759.
81. This was an amazing figure considering that there were only 2,228 adult males in Ashford according to census data.
82. "Statue of Colonel Thomas Knowlton, Ceremonies at the Unveiling." This unattributable quote appears inside this catalogue.
83. This is how Washington described the Battle of Harlem Heights in a letter to the president of the Continental Congress, John Hancock, dated September 18, 1776. George Washington Papers, Library of Congress.
84. "Statue of Colonel Thomas Knowlton, Ceremonies at the Unveiling."
85. Just miles from both spots rest the remains of his grandnephew, General Nathaniel Lyon, the first Union general to be killed in the American Civil War.
86. "Thomas Knowlton," en.wikipedia.org.

Chapter 7

87. Flexnor, *George Washington*.
88. On February 19, 1777, Thomas Mifflin, Arthur St. Clair, William Alexander (Lord Stirling), Adam Stephen and Benjamin Lincoln were promoted.
89. Arnold married Margaret Mansfield in 1767. They had three sons. Arnold was thirty-eight when he married Peggy Shippen. Having not received a salary in years, Arnold had to personally underwrite his lifestyle.
90. See the Library of Congress, Washington's General Orders, April 6, 1780, for a review. Congress heard eight charges of misconduct against Arnold and then exonerated him, but Reed obtained a reconsideration, and in April 1779, Congress, though throwing out four charges, referred the other four to a court-martial.
91. His brother Benedict Arnold IV died during childhood. Only he and sister Hannah survived until adulthood.
92. See the Clements Library, University of Michigan, letters from Arnold to André, July 12, 1780, and July 15, 1780. Arnold's spouse, Peggy, also acted as a willing intermediary.
93. With West Point—a place Arnold valued at £20,000—in their possession, the British would have controlled the critical Hudson River Valley and

separated New England from the rest of the colonies. It was the first and last meeting between André and Arnold. One of Arnold's Tory friends would escort André through part of his journey. Tallmadge had heard rumors through his intelligence lattice of a high-ranking traitor and the name Anderson through the turncoat himself. Washington's network also detected signs of British battle preparation.

94. Washington, Henry Knox, Lafayette and aide Colonel Alexander Hamilton arrived not knowing the cause of Arnold's absence.

95. Washington's exact words have also been questioned.

96. Sergeant John Champe, agent Allan McLane and Governor Thomas Jefferson all failed in their attempt to kidnap Arnold.

97. Arnold abandoned the morals, principles and beliefs that the Revolution represented. His demonization, to some, has been deemed unfair as it overshadows his contributions to American independence.

CHAPTER 8

98. The preeminent figure of the American Enlightenment, Benjamin Franklin was among the most famous and lionized men of the world.

99. *Encyclopaedia Britannica.* Sources vary regarding Bancroft's date of birth and date of death.

100. In 1769, Bancroft also published a pro-American pamphlet that attracted a great deal of attention for its views on Parliament's claim to colonial jurisdiction.

101. Bancroft also used additional and much safer methods of communication.

102. Ironically, when Deane was recalled by Congress in 1778, it was Bancroft, a man who hadn't missed a word from Deane's mouth or pen, who affirmed his diligent public service. Some view Bancroft as a spy but not a traitor. See Samuel Flagg Bemis, "British Secret Service and the French-American Alliance," *American Historical Review* 29 (April 1924).

103. Schiff, *A Great Improvisation*, 238. There were times when Franklin felt relieved by Bancroft's presence, like when he feared being poisoned by schemer Peter Allaire. Both Franklin and Bancroft sought a charter for land along the Ohio River. Bancroft and Deane also speculated in the London insurance markets.

CHAPTER 9

104. Bushnell's description of the submarine and "Other Experiments" was first published in *Transactions of the American Philosophical Society* (Philadelphia, 1799).

105. His classmates included Nathan Hale and diplomat Joel Barlow. These design requirements were set forth by the United Sates Navy.

106. *Dr. James Thacher's Military Journal of the American Revolution* (Hartford, CT: American Subscription House, 1862).

107. Deane, *Correspondence of Silas Deane,* 315–18.

108. Diamant, *Chaining the Hudson,* 26. Though the details were inaccurate, the device had been acknowledged.

109. Hoadly, *Public Records of Connecticut,* 15:232–34.

110. George Washington to Thomas Jefferson, Mount Vernon, September 26, 1785, in *The Papers of Thomas Jefferson,* 13:555–57.

111. Bushnell's description of the submarine and "Other Experiments" was published in *Transactions of the American Philosophical Society.*

112. Ibid.

113. Ibid.

114. Ibid.

115. Ibid.

116. David Humphreys—a Revolutionary War colonel and aide-de-camp to George Washington—was enjoying his retirement years as an author.

117. *Dr. James Thacher's Military Journal of the American Revolution* (Hartford, CT: American Subscription House, 1862).

118. Ibid.

119. Inside the museum you will not only find a replica of Bushnell's *Turtle* but outside, and equally as impressive, rests the first nuclear-powered submarine, the USS *Nautilus.*

CHAPTER 10

120. It was a gamble as espionage had not yet been examined in popular fiction.

121. Barnum, *The Spy Unmasked,* 46.

122. Since in all of America there had been but seven presses issuing newspapers before 1750, information, especially accurate accounts, was seldom timely.

123. The document—in support of his application for a federal pension, which had just been made available through an act of Congress (passed June 7, 1832)—resides with the New York State Historical Association. It appeared in *New York History* XLVII, no. 1 (January 1966): 61–73.

124. Barnum, *The Spy Unmasked.*

125. The Committee for Detecting Conspiracies must have learned either from Captain Townsend or from the Committee at White Plains.

126. The Committee for Detecting Conspiracies indemnified Crosby from his enlistment.

127. The company planned to travel to New York to join the British army.

128. Crosby had been employed in the Secret Service for nine months.

129. *Putnam Courier,* June 26, 1914. Crosby had two sons and four daughters, all from Sarah Kniffen Nickerson, his first wife, who died in 1811. His second spouse, whom he married about 1824, died in 1828 and was buried in Somers, New York, next to her first husband, Colonel Benjamin George. Later, Enoch Crosby with his brother Benjamin bought a farm in the town of Southeast and lived there until he died on June 26, 1835. The Enoch Crosby Chapter of the Daughters of the American Revolution continues to play an active role in Putnam County.

CHAPTER 11

130. Phelps, *Nathan Hale.*

131. George Washington Papers, Library of Congress. Letter dated September 6, 1776.

132. Account by Reverend Edward Everett Hale (EEH).

133. A position set forth in his personal correspondence and confirmed in Captain Hull's memoirs.

134. Root, *True Stories of Great Americans.*

135. Ibid.

136. Ibid. Referencing Captain Hull's memoirs.

137. Ibid.

138. Ibid.

139. The mission left about September 12, 1776. Departing from Norwalk, the landing is believed to have taken place three days later. The shoe buckles are now property of the Nathan Hale Homestead. The British seized New York City on September 15, 1776. Countering, the American

commander-in-chief opted for a position of strength at Fort Washington on the other end of the island. The following morning, Washington ordered the Connecticut Rangers "to gain intelligence if possible of the disposition of the enemy." It would be during this mission that Colonel Knowlton would fall, mortally wounded.

140. Edward Everett Hale believed only in his account. Consider Tiffany, a Connecticut shopkeeper and Loyalist, believed Colonel Robert Rogers, who was in the area, recognized Hale and gained a mission confession and that Hale's identity was confirmed by others calling him by name. Samuel Hale, a cousin, was General William Howe's deputy commissary of prisoners. Some believe he may also have been involved.

141. McCullough, *1776*, 224.

142. Root, *True Stories of Great Americans*, referencing Captain Hull's memoirs, according to Bakeless in *Turncoats, Traitors & Heroes*, 120. Cunningham himself was hanged for forgery in London.

143. Ibid. Letters believed to be to his brother Enoch and his commanding officer. Cunningham commanded possession of the correspondence.

144. Author M. William Phelps quotes a different line found in the *Essex Journal*, February 2, 1777, published in Newburyport, Massachusetts.

145. Letter from Nathan Hale to Dr. Aeneas Munson at New Haven, November 30, 1774. Yale classmate Benjamin Tallmadge was also a teacher and friend of Hale.

146. Ibid.

147. Root, *True Stories of Great Americans*. Letter from Nathan Hale to the proprietors of Union High School, New London.

148. It was during the Siege of Boston that Washington first took note of Hale.

149. A twist from Thomas Paine's *The American Crisis*. The British had broken the first rule of engagement: never provoke or inspirit your enemy.

CHAPTER 12

150. Described to writer Washington Irving by eyewitnesses. Irving, in *The Life of George Washington*, also claimed the leader "wept with the tenderness of a child."

151. Letter from George Washington to Nathaniel Sackett, February 4, 1777. International Spy Museum, 800 F Street NW, Washington, D.C.,

20004. Washington agreed to pay Sackett $50 per month plus $500 to set up his spy network.

152. Tallmadge also tutored in Wethersfield, Connecticut—home to Silas Deane.

153. A comprehensive listing of Washington's headquarters is available from the University of Virginia–Charlottesville.

154. Upon her husband's release, with which Anna assisted, the family spent the remainder of the war in Connecticut.

155. Historian Catherine Snell Crary claimed that Rivington spied for Washington.

156. Bakeless, *Turncoats, Traitors & Heroes*, 228–29. Connecticut, although not impervious to espionage, was one of the safer legs of the journey. According to Bakeless, some missives were uncoded in ordinary ink and went through the hands of Israel Putnam.

157. Washington also wouldn't hesitate to use Tallmadge as a case officer.

158. Some remember Mulligan for tearing down the statue of King George II in New York's Bowling Green Park. Alexander Hamilton, who once boarded with the Mulligans, told Washington of his friend.

159. The Culpers did not receive pay and did not always collect compensation for their expenses. Tallmadge himself lost a saddlebag—inside the bag were covert missives, including one from Washington himself—when he was attacked by British troops.

160. The British dispatched agent Nehemiah Marks. Believing in the existence of the network, Marks recommended to the British to wait, gather more intelligence and then capture the suspects. However, a plan was never enacted.

161. Comprehensive handwriting analysis, conducted in 1939 under the watchful eye of historian Morton Pennypacker, revealed that Culper Jr. was indeed Robert Townsend. Graphologist Albert S. Osborn was retained to make the determination. Sally Townsend, sister of Culper Jr., is a character of interest in Bakeless, *Turncoats, Traitors & Heroes*, 290–91.

162. The original location of Austin Roe's tavern was along what is now Route 25A in East Setauket. It was moved in 1936.

163. Woodhull referred to 355 only one other time and not by name. Most Washington biographers give no credence to the reference beyond the obvious. Many British troops were quartered in the homes of Long Island residents.

Bibliography

ARTICLES

Crews, Ed. "Spies and Scouts, Secret Writing, and Sympathetic Citizens." *Colonial Williamsburg Journal*, Summer 2004.

Gerlander, Todd L. "Understanding the Connecticut Militia During the American Revolution." New England Contingent Sons of the American Revolution, 2010.

Hutson, James. "Nathan Hale Revisited: A Tory's Account of the Arrest of the First American Spy." *The Library of Congress* 62, no. 7 (July/August 2003).

Wilcox, Jennifer. "Revolutionary Secrets: The Secret Communications of the American Revolution." http://www.nsa.gov/about/_files/cryptologic_heritage/publications/prewii/Revolutionary_Secrets.pdf.

CATALOGUES

"Connecticut in the American Revolution." An exhibition from the Library and Museum Collections of the Society of the Cincinnati, Anderson House, Washington, D.C., October 27, 2001–May 11, 2002.

"Spy Letters of the American Revolution." From the collection of the Clements Library.

"Statue of Colonel Thomas Knowlton, Ceremonies at the Unveiling."
Hartford, CT: Press of the Case, Lockwood & Brainard Company, 1895.

PHOTOGRAPHS

Any photograph followed by a LC-, HABS or GWP is courtesy of the Library
of Congress. All other photograph sources are identified or property of the
author. A special acknowledgement to the Connecticut River Museum, the
National Portrait Gallery and the White House Historical Association, as
well as to the town of Coventry, Connecticut. Collage on page 126: BT,
LC-USZ62-59149,GW by Rembrandt Peale, BF, LC-USZC4-11045, CM,
LC-Gm70002894M.

INTERNET SITES

American Ancestors, New England Historic Genealogical Society, www.
   american ancestors.org.
Ancestry.com
The Connecticut Society of the Daughters of the American Revolution,
   www.ctdar.org.
The Connecticut Society of the Sons of the American Revolution, www.
   connecticutsar.org.
International Spy Museum, www.spymuseum.org.
The Joseph Bucklin Society, www.bucklinsociety.com.
The Library of Congress, www.loc.gov.
National Archives and Records Administration (NARA), www.archives.gov.
National Security Agency (NSA), www.nsa.gov.
New York Public Library, www.nypl.org.
Revolutionary Connecticut, www.revolutionaryct.com.
Silas Deane Online, www.silasdeaneonline.org.
The Society of Cincinnati, www.societyofthecincinnati.org.
State University of New York College–Oneonta (SUNY–Oneonta), Cooper
   Society, external.oneonta.edu/cooper.
United Empire Loyalists' Association of Canada, www.uelac.org.
United States Army, www.army.mil.

United States Department of Veterans Affairs, www.va.gov.
University of Connecticut Libraries, www.lib.uconn.edu
University of Michigan, Clements Library, www.clements.umich.edu.
Wikipedia, www.wikipedia.org.

BOOKS

Allen, Ethan. *A Narrative of Col. Ethan Allen's Captivity*. Philadelphia: Robert Bell, 1779.

Allen, Thomas B. *George Washington, Spymaster: How the Americans Outspied the British and Won the Revolutionary War*. Washington, D.C.: National Geographic, 2004.

Axelrod, Alan. *The American Revolution, What Really Happened*. New York: Fall River Press, 2007.

Babcock, James Staunton. *Memoir of Nathan Hale*. New Haven, CT: S. Babcock, 1844.

Bakeless, John. *Turncoats, Traitors & Heroes: Espionage in the American Revolution*. New York: Da Capo Press Edition, 1998.

Barnum, H.L. *The Spy Unmasked; or, Memoirs of Enoch Crosby, alias Harvey Birch*. New York: J.&J. Harper, Cliff-Street, 1829.

Botkin, B.A. *A Treasury of New England Folklore*. Rev. ed. New York: American Legacy Press, 1965.

Boudinot, J.J., ed. *The Life, Public Services, Addresses and Letters of Elias Boudinot*. New York: Houghton, Mifflin and Company, 1896.

Chernow, Ron. *Washington: A Life*. New York: Penguin Press, 2010.

Clark, George L. *Silas Deane: A Connecticut Leader in the American Revolution*. New York: G.P. Putnam's Sons, 1913.

Deane, Silas. *Correspondence of Silas Deane Delegate to the Congress at Philadelphia, 1774–1776*. Collections of the Connecticut Historical Society. Hartford, CT, 1860–62.

Diamant, Lincoln. *Chaining the Hudson: The Fight for the River in the American Revolution*. New York: Fordham University Press, 2004.

Flexnor, James Thomas. *George Washington*. 4 vols. Boston: Little Brown, 1965–72.

Franklin, Benjamin. "The Morals of Chess." In Walker, George. *The Chess Player*. Boston: Dearborn, 1841.

Goodrich, Samuel Griswold. *Curiosities of Human Nature*. Boston: Bradbury, Soden & Company, 1844.

Hale, Edward Everett. *Capt. Nathan Hale, An Address Delivered at Groton, Connecticut, on the Hale Memorial Day, September 7, 1881.* Boston: A Williams & Company, 1881.

Hoadly, Charles T. *The Public Records of the Colony of Connecticut.* Hartford, CT: Press of the Case, Lockwood and Brainard Co., 1850–90.

Irving, Washington. *The Life of George Washington.* New York: William L. Allison Co., 1859.

Jefferson, Thomas. *The Papers of Thomas Jefferson.* Edited by Julian Boyd et al. 34 vols. Princeton, NJ: Princeton University Press, 1950–58.

Livingston, William Farrand. *Israel Putnam, Pioneer, Ranger, and Major General, 1718–1790.* New York: G.P. Putnam's Sons, 1901.

McCullough, David. *John Adams.* New York: Simon & Schuster, 2001.

———. *1776.* New York: Simon & Schuster, 2005.

Paul, Joel Richard. *Unlikely Allies: How a Merchant, a Playwright, and a Spy Saved the American Revolution.* New York: Riverhead Books, 2009.

Phelps, M. William. *Nathan Hale: The Life and Times of America's First Spy.* New York: Thomas Dunn Books, St. Martin's Press, 2008.

Phelps, Noah A. *History of Simsbury, Granby and Canton, from 1642 to 1845.* Hartford, CT: Press of Case, Tiffany and Burnham, 1845.

Phillips, Kevin. *1775: A Good Year for Revolution.* New York: Viking, 2012.

Randall, William Sterne. *Ethan Allen: His Life and Times.* New York: W.W. Norton & Company, 2011.

Raphael, Ray. *Founding Myths, Stories That Hide Our Patriotic Past.* New York: MJF Books, 2004.

Root, Jean Christie. *Nathan Hale.* New York: MacMillan Company, 1915.

Schaeper, Thomas. *Edward Bancroft: Scientist, Author, Spy.* New Haven, CT: Yale University Press, 2011.

Schiff, Stacy. *A Great Improvisation, Franklin, France, and the Birth of America.* New York: Henry Holt and Company, 2005.

Sparks, Jared. *The Life of Col. Ethan Allen.* Burlington, VT: C.Goodrich & Company, 1858.

Stiles, Henry R. *The History and Genealogies of Ancient Windsor, Connecticut (1635–1891).* Vol. I. Hartford, CT: Press of the Case, Lockwood & Brainard Company, 1891.

Stone, Reverend Chas. E. *Simsbury's Part in the War of the American Revolution.* Hartford, CT: Press of the Case, Lokwood & Brainard Company, 1896.

Thacher, Dr. James. *Dr. James Thacher's Military Journal of the American Revolution.* Hartford, CT: American Subscription House, 1862.

Trumbull, John. *Autobiography, Reminiscences and Letters of John Trumbull, from 1756 to 1841.* New York: Wiley and Putnam, 1841.

Trumbull, Jonathan. *Jonathan Trumbull, Governor of Connecticut, 1769–1784.* Boston: Little, Brown, and Company, 1919.

Wain, Robert. *Biography of the Signers of the Declaration of Independence.* Philadelphia: R.W. Pomeroy, 1827.

Washington, George. *Accounts, G. Washington with the United States, Commencing June 1775, and Ending June 1783, Comprehending a Space of 8 Years.* Washington, D.C.: Library of Congress.

Woodward, Ashbel. *Memoir of Col. Thomas Knowlton of Ashford, Connecticut.* Boston: Henry W. Dutton & Son, 1861.

CRYPTOGRAM EXERCISE

Test your code breaking skills on the following cryptograms:

1.) R hIZZJHXtHiX HIZlZyalE
   Hint: Silas Deane

2.) VNPNfRKbI VNKRnB wT "AGN PBNNf HWlFAKJF YWIZ"
   Hint: Ethan Allen

3.) NIZBHTN'd UHBDo HSoZAAHEZStZ JBQUZDDHQSNA
   Hint: Thomas Knowlton

4.) IYBWXWB ZPMYMPoYJZ RCFQ FBTCFYB
   Hint: Benedict Arnold

5.) YRNJTKXWXRG IMR UnI TW IMR JYZ
   Hint: Edward Bancroft

6.) "Q oXI DS KUY UQZL oUYZZ"
   Hint: David Bushnell & Ezra Lee

7.) J oMl, CX GaZ "ZWK"
   Hint: Enoch Crosby

8.) "CeF" UICZYPC
   Hint: Nathan Hale

9.) 8-a-26-f,a, 25-18-11-25-8, 6-13, 20-4-25-5-3, a,15-18-5-a-25, 26-6-5.
   Hint: Quote

10.) vbwu jel ubemm vbqw aq eph pq jwlvbil! vbepo sqw jql liehcpa.
   Hint: The Culper Ring

The answers are listed on the following page. Don't peek!

Answers to coded messages (1 though 8): 1. A Connecticut Conundrum; 2. Legendary Leader of "The Green Mountain Boys"; 3. America's First Intelligence Professional; 4. Forever Synonymous with Traitor; 5. Personified the Art of the Spy; 6. "A Spy on the Half Shell"; 7. A Spy, if not "The"; 8. "The" Patriot.; 9. Half a truth is often a great lie.; 10. Thus Far Shall Thou Go and No Further!

Thank you for reading.

Index

About the Author

M ark Allen Baker is a former business executive (assistant to the president and CEO at General Electric, Genigraphics Corporation, a former division of General Electric—now Microsoft PowerPoint) and entrepreneur. As an author of seventeen books, including the award-nominated *Title Town USA: Boxing in Upstate New York* and *Basketball History in Syracuse: Hoops Roots*, and historian, his expertise has been referenced in numerous periodicals, including *USA TODAY*, *Sports Illustrated* and *Money*. Appearing on numerous radio and televisions shows, Baker was also a co-host on *Rock Collectors*, a VH1 television series.

The author can be contacted at: PO Box 782, Hebron, Connecticut, 06248.